"...BUT I COULD NOT SPEAK..."

"...But I Could Not Speak..."

·] ·] ·] [· [· [·

JONO SCHNEIDER

O Books · 2002

Parts of this manuscript have previously appeared in *Untitled*, *Hambone*, and *Fiasco*. The author thanks the editors for their support. The author gives special thanks to Leonard Brink, Andrew Felsinger, Gil Ott, Ethan Paquin, Sarah Rosenthal, and Ben Steiner for their continually careful reading of his work.

Cover design and photographs: Leslie Scalapino
Typesetting and design: Guy Bennett

ISBN: 1-882022-45-9
Library of Congress Control Number: 2002107813

"Speak, man!" said Captain Vere to the transfixed one, struck by his aspect even more than Claggart's. "Speak! Defend yourself!" Which appeal caused but a strange dumb gesturing and gurgling in Billy; amazement at such an accusation so suddenly sprung on inexperienced nonage; this, and, it may be, horror of the accuser's eyes, serving to bring out his lurking defect and in this instance for the time intensifying it into a convulsed tongue-tie; while the intent head and entire form straining forward in an agony of ineffectual eagerness to obey the injunction to speak and defend himself, gave an expression to the face like that of a condemned vestal priestess in the moment of being buried alive, and in the first struggle against suffocation.

– HERMAN MELVILLE,
Billy Budd

But I couldn't speak. There were many people around me, none of whom I knew. Night approached. I couldn't see the horizon until someone lit a torch, perhaps too soon for anyone to accurately speak of it. The noise seemed endless (now I think of it); I recognized a sign that I had passed as the road and the sky (not in succession). The bugs, the ants, were insatiable, were inscrutable, crawling among all our possessions: yet only this would cure me. The silence was an achievement of privacy as I became acutely restrained by it. Was this the present in front of me?

"Don't cry out," I cautioned. All was impossible to identify. The wings hit the air, and I wished for rain – but this would not be my form of prayer. Were the clouds here to help harvest the resolute silence of the rest?

The man turned towards the boy, his son, after burning himself. The tightness continued to grow. And I removed myself as the support. His movements resembled the sound of a pencil, as water had now become available everywhere. "If you want to move, there are places which will always seek you out in return." I was now ready to finally give advice. Things were happening too slowly for us to simply understand them as we saw them, and it was difficult for everyone to continue without substantial and permanent revision. And yet time was further than the truth content of any given statement that might have entered the room by way of what I may have said in there. Sure, the dogs would not catch me, but I was no less nervous as I heard them becoming more restless in the distance. I wrote that because the distance was not as you might think, was not even as far as the word or as far as the word makes it out to be. I wasn't able to designate my attention; I was unfashionably fixed by my lack of it. The future was forewarned by those I no longer knew. I could say no more about each creature that crawled on me and how they did so, for I was to invent something very soon and needed my energy to form a fist. Yes, the sky was open to us, but only as an interpretation, as it still would not address my proposals, which I silently composed in honor of the night that would make its final arrival.

The sheet covered the ground, and a root protruded out of the ground.

I would read no more letters this evening until I had finished; excitement pushed me to think in advance of the words, an inaccurate meaning carrying my failures forward. Something appeared as a smell, eroded that of my fingers. I cannot tell you that the people had formed a circle. But I had lost more weight than I had written. The noises extended the questions into the distance; this accentuated our approach and coincided with any new opportunities I might have been able to salvage, save and have for myself. And I established questions; for example: "When should I have the lights turned on as the horizon becomes more or less visible before my expertise?"

I was uncertain of the downstroke, so speech did not enter on a silver platter. Here the ground was laid sadly to rest. Heat does not boggle the mind so much as wither it, I thought. The look on her face seemed to vacillate between happiness and indecision, but this is not for me to say as I sit here and fake my way through the act of interpretation. I was still uncertain if the composition, on a larger scale than the sentence, was historical when its formal concerns, though unannounced, were not that of the present because the words were formed out of a precise loyalty to meaning as a specificity that exhausts the act of writing. "Caution," I would later say, my face marked with ink, "is not a property of feeling, but of unconvinced action." This time I swore that I would no longer work like a slave to the age; I would finally move forth by ignoring the paper supply.

The door has closed, and I never heard it closing. "Father and son drew no closer in the wake of the man's pain because they quickly turned the tragedy into a reaction around which their relationship formed a silent pact" – he did not say this to me but for self-knowledge. Everything interested me when the sky's brightness coincided with rhythms that did not name the time. Simulation was an inevitability when staring at these two men: one (father) who bends over, another (son) who skips in place with a bulge. She refuses my blindness. This is what causes her own pain. "I do not desire these repetitions," I whispered.

He was wearing a sheet so that I could see little of him, but enough was made clear to me by the way in which he held his face away from the light. I could hear objectivity against the background of the day that we were ready to discuss. We had come to this point, in which simultaneity was the result of trying to speed up our actions, and our actions no longer meant the things that had required us to think of changing ourselves. But then, I have never changed myself according to a plan that I could then reiterate by describing, one that asserts itself all the more the less I allow myself to listen to it.

"A coordinator locks truth in more firmly, challenging falsehood to rise once again and dance more furiously in front of the leaping fire than before" – she was at my heels with liberties like these.

Such statements needed to be crossed out but could not be relinquished for fear that too few words would cover the page, making what had been retained sadly assume a greater importance than had been intended, and yet this loss of control yielded a variety of meaning that I have not yet been determined by although I'm being written out in it.

The horizon had nothing to do with us. I chose to ignore safety for safety reasons; my preference was to erase its resonance as we gathered with ease around the ranger who let the distance provide the silence with its sober tone. "Ever the musical economizer," I quipped, but couldn't so much as evoke a slight smirk from the ranger. "One more line will end the world" – this is a form of saying too much to fill space that may never have been empty and now is surely no longer.

I rolled over and rubbed myself to taunt fate, which had been waiting for me forever with conditions whose originality would turn the moment into an awakening. I seemed similarly aware when I finally found myself turning around and closing my eyes. And I was not operating in relation to a complex game of chance.

The message angered me by pushing the ability to be creative while sitting against the wall away from me, and I knew that I would be called into action much sooner than I was ready because the proposal would not clear a confident path to action. I must always tell myself how hollow it all sounds; "Hollow is the repetition as it is sounded out," is the actual order of the words I use to say this.

I knew that knowing no one would eventually catch up with me. I could instruct myself only slightly in the rules that, having written them out for me, she had eternally foresworn. "The wind does blow, but it requires that you stand still," I opined. But I still had many available options with relation to what I wanted her to hear me say.

The man ate quietly and quickly because it seemed as if he enjoyed hurrying as an excuse against what it might have meant at that moment for him to kick back (but not the can). Yet I do not know what a template for rushing resembles as it is formed in a sluggish paragraph. The same visual image has left me alone with this sentence. Will his death end up as slowly as this sentence has?

No first step availed itself to us until we had pieced it together from scraps laid out on the rug, but these stabs at reality were not provided for us unless we diligently reinforced them. The window did not click like I had hoped and banged in the next room instead. I inquired: "Is the driving force of a novel the creation of its characters, or is it within them?"

"Whether or not I am willing to risk myself among others to do something equally valid for all" is the only phrase that speaks of my precise locative abilities. If I had not put myself there, I would not think about it for fear of losing the idea propelling action as an option. But writing is not in opposition to action. I chewed on the cap, a nervous tic which I usually hide, but I wanted to show that my anxiety could reach its peak if pushed.

The debate about what makes a narrative compelling is contingent upon the amount of truth the narrative says it reports to the reader only if that reader expects that learning the relation between the narrative and the truth will change life for a moment – even if this change is false when applied to the moment of narration.

Anxiety is my ungainly misfortune. The horizon's anxiety appears with the sun and disappears with the clouds that shield it from us. I lose my visibility in it. This is a way for me to combine psychology with saying how easily personification is protection against indifference. I slept and she drew more quietly. It was swiftly becoming gray.

"I don't want to write, but I am afraid of what will happen to me if I don't," I admitted.

The boy did not see what happened to his father from the angle that I saw it; this meant that he did not know how the words looked coming off of the man's lips.

The ugliness was sufficient for us to decide to leave, as it exploded into the air with a force that we would have embraced had we been more knowledgeable of how to interrupt its technique with our own force. It is for lack of force that I enter the space, and yet I do not enter it, for the words surround it. Less language did not explain the sentiment with a fury that was derivative of others. To the left is emptiness, a whimper no longer in the distance.

Ants were an intricate part of the machinery that beckoned us to look longer than we planned. He scaled the rock and failed to prove that action was effective as a means of silent force, telling me to keep my distance only when I began the day by being distant. Moving down leads me ahead of myself. I said better things long ago, and now I have forgetting to write them.

I find the way as easy as opening a file, as difficult as putting my fingers down. Here I want to use the word "detective," but, being embarrassed, I back away from this. Our pact breaks off when the strap begins to falter.

Unlocked, a door worked in vain to prove protection to us. The first page suggested sentences that were infrequent, and therefore original enough to repeat as an alternate route ahead of me. She didn't agree that the words were humorous or ridiculous – I was mired in insecurity and could only explain things through a lens that wasn't necessarily destructive. But it may have also alienated me from habits, originality now meaning "a beginning that does not begin with you". Who was it that told me to be silent in writing? Who am I if I feel silence but do not fall into it?

A feeling was the most passionate answer I could promise her of the scene that held too many memories for me to tell her about myself and how I had handled what at the time seemed impossible, that now seems even less possible, for my forgetfulness shows me the likelihood of events whose occurrences are solved in me. Distance was formulated by a question and demanded we disconnect. The air paused in its ignorance of these occurrences. To be sure, I moved backwards and saw that although I had done more than speak, I had not yet acted. "Rhythms are a subtle addiction," I mused. But it was place that had confirmed these reservations, our limits of behavior. No, we did not want such an outcome as this. Was that how my body would also end – in ethics?

It was not so much that I wanted to fit in – rather, I sought the effects of putting myself in line to receive the kind of comments I could easily decode, so that, in fact, it would no longer be necessary for me to wonder what had been said. He could now read the signs with ease and not repeat them to the persons on his left.

I left nothing behind; because of this, I found myself having difficulty doing small things. "It is the paper's fault, not the mind's, that it has become more challenging to act in such a way so that my interest fully blossoms" – I was once again involved in analysis. This diversion was necessary for me to become used to to once again see the sky as something that was complete in its independence from me.

This man was one whom I would never know. His sequence didn't seek to teach me. By sequestering him next door, she accidentally let me try to accomplish a phrase before it became too late.

Would history have helped the one who wrote it to know more about each person the story had introduced into the world, or was it more likely that novels had never made introductions as clear as they were presented in poems, where objects and people were as interchangeable in space as words?

A space cleared my mind long enough for other faces to enter it and change it once again. So I was denied a chance to close my eyes and wonder. Time didn't disappoint me but restructured the moment by distancing it from pleasure. That was not an echo – unless it resurfaces.

I was still waiting and would continue on in this way indefinitely, indestructibly. The words were the winds that had blown us far from each other because we couldn't understand them; we could not apply their strict scrutiny directly to our lives. We would need a sentence to contain pleasure while acknowledging the pain we had come through to move down the unimaginable line we still draw. I mouthed. The silence was proclaimed in the heat that showed us its relentlessness, so we moved away from one another as it correlated its increase with the oncoming darkness. I then asked, "How can you stop what prompts you without moving yourself as it does?"

What was possible wasn't always what this now is contained in. I tried not to think about what I had been doing to hold back the nostalgia keeping me from forming what I immediately understood as worthy of my time. Yet I could not articulate this as the sum total of an aesthetic project whose grand gesture I was now able to announce by repeating the context that had created it.

To right myself before the next entry, I lifted my head forward and saw new things which adjusted the pause of speaking into the time of written speech. Both were equal to remaining absolute in my silence. So I would permanently break into sections. I've thought more about the night since I last spoke of it and now think that "approach" is too awkward a term to write because it implies a direct object that is always present in the sentence even if it is not actually written in it. This presence assumes we exist before stating it. But metaphysics does not transcend us.

The categories "novel" and "poem" leave historical traces behind us. Now it is up to narrative – or at least to me who is claiming this by writing to it – to rekindle the assimilation of characteristics that we have become thoroughly aware of as long as we continue to read critiques of what builds up the world into philosophy.

She entered the bathroom long enough for me to realize she was no longer sleeping. I was behind her. We did not greet each other. The market was crowded (I did not think this but I am now outside of it), and it is behind the "I am."

Deciding between eating, waiting, and writing complicated the afternoon, which was nearly over and had hardly produced all that to which I had become habitually accustomed. "I do not yet yearn," I hissed.

An animal was attached to her finger; she accentuated this connection by shaking and laughing when everyone looked at it. Afterwards we assiduously checked our words for bugs.

How heavy would the book I needed to read to change the past into an open room be? If only I had said that to her as an advertisement of my love for others. The words I had used appalled her because of the amount of letters they held in common, and she urged me to "change them or else familiarity would reign too freely." Our philosophic consultation resulted in our being together all afternoon.

Are all the beset reactions repeating themselves for her alone?

The boy hadn't shown us any new signs. And water was not simplified matter – we had only begun to learn the axioms and translate them into usable truths.

It seemed to me that I would need to bring a notebook to apply myself to the project that I would be unable to imagine. I became aware of this only when I began to worry about how I would handle myself over the next two weeks, which were not, as you might think, so much filled with obstacles as with attempts to venture further into repetition as an indentation that confirmed my stylistic identity.

She was very close to returning until I gently convinced her. Being flattered by her second offer could not shield my disappointment at her initial snub, which hung over every interaction between us. And yet I understood him. "I don't want to be at home," I quipped. So as not to have to judge him, I didn't ask her about him.

It was not speech that turned silence into such a radical proposal, but silence as we had redirected it into an essential part of the game of chance we played with one another when we looked at each other and guessed what the other was feeling from the look on her face. Their faces didn't teach us how to know them any better. This number was not emphasized. The end flickered against the distance that seemed to rise behind it and divide the importance between us into modes by which we could have understood each other if we had remained with the sun in our eyes for no more than a minute longer. Telling a story was perhaps to perpetrate it with our existence; this did not mean we knew anything more than the exact instant which propelled us to say to ourselves that we wanted to add its existence to what we knew of ourselves prior to it. And yet I was needed, was in need. These ideas do not link us to each other by likeness. Afterwards, I found I had only to push down to predict what could come after the very things that I thought had confronted me with the facets of a distance I would never outgrow. I was of no moods, distributed among many bodies.

I had reached the horizon through work. Alone on that morning, nothing could teach me about how fate operated until I found my way to the exit and felt how serious the wind was when it whipped. And she hadn't left her sentiments in back because errands would have made her concentrate all of her energy upon me as if I was a single point made to clinch an argumentative pennant.

It is across the street. I have never gone that far, which does not mean that I have been afraid. My curiosity is something I have yet to reach.

The dream spoke to me of everything I wished I had brought back with me so I wouldn't have to face the fact that such ideas remained out-of-print, and, as a matter of convenience, unreadable when I became aware that I was missing them. Reading the phrase "gone missing" as a question did not invite my interest as a social phenomenon; I was diverted instead towards rules which provided the ground for public stoicism. "I am against all silence," I retorted.

Finding a cure became an opportunity for me to continue to look and satisfied my restless need for change, but it also invited more unanswerable questions from others at whom, had I been given a reason to speak of them, I would have projected a silence that proved my distance through an anger that was not a clearly pronounced set of directions. But it was writing that alienated me by amazing them because its power was not one I had ever focused sincerely.

Power is a kindred spell of stillness. Though the sky still did not recognize me, I wanted to use their advisement when I spoke to it. Was this discontinuation?

The man and boy couldn't count this recollection as an effort to get to know each other in a revolutionary way, for they were still standing in the same places when they spoke to each other as before, and the room grew no smaller because of the words they used. Distance was now more present than ever before because it did not leave them to each other, and, as they had persuaded each other that intimacy was a material fact they could measure through conversation, neither of them, had they been asked to point to its current location, could have said where the intimacy was buried in the room. Fiction was therefore an essential property I would always have to keep in front of me so as not to lose my way along the axis that language had laid out so exquisitely before me. This was to say everything in history. Metaphysics did not rise to a higher level than the evidence I was writing.

I would soon have to improve upon the fastener to make use easier and show favors to the anonymous user. It was in the future that I had decided the form; only later could I see the potentialities that I now had, now that I had remade myself through the process of art, a process which I wouldn't proclaim to the world until I was sure that that was what I had, indeed, experienced. "This mess doesn't describe me," I agreed; I was swiftly decoding the experience for myself at home. This seemed natural enough, but could not serve as my final justification.

She wanted space in order to provoke new memory, even if this was a short cut. She sounded like someone else when she spoke intimately of how she intensely disfigured herself. And we were content but lonely when the sun caved in against the horizon.

It has been too long since I let the dogs find me; I had sworn that the owners would not forget my pain so quickly. The odd page did not report itself to me, instead seeming to arise when I looked directly at it longer than I intended.

·] 22

She told me to go as far as I possibly could, and not to stop when it looked like there was no alternative because, she argued, that was the moment when everything was ready to break down and actually become something unknown to each of us. She knew this to be art. If I truly wished to reinforce the importance of my relationship to it, I could do nothing bolder than risk myself among it by destroying myself in making it. Were "the dogs" the names by which I used to exalt creativity when I was urged not to do so?

Buzzing with a ferocity that startled us into attending to its every movement and that told us our responsibility to it, the machine made us feel content with ourselves.

As I plucked it out of the air that I was going to give to her, my happiness didn't guide me but belonged instead to that lengthy decision we availed ourselves to make. She waited for sounds to take her to the sea without telling me how her silence would keep all enough intact for us to listen to her again. It wasn't a repetition when she first spit it into the sea.

They asked for more from the other than it was possible for each of them to give, being dependent upon each other. They were overburdened with the ongoing project of inching ahead because they had not fully accepted the pasts that contained their present identities. These were the very identities that had brought them to examine each other so closely. But their aching eyes were hardly able to search over the signals much longer.

I was not at an advantage by being knowledgable of things that I couldn't apply unless I changed the subject and therefore showed my limitations. "You are your own argument," I impressed. The silence I was returned was multi-tiered. My body won't come back with me when I return, however hard it pulls me away from knowledge because of the pains that have resurfaced.

We had sealed it with tape too thick to puncture, causing me to forget the favor I had asked for and rethink an aimless agenda based upon meaningful whims. But it is certain that the intelligence displayed in the room cannot be divided into columns.

That it was no longer a novel but a voice – a voice whose speech did not name the character who spoke it, instead letting it issue forth a flow of words attached to the conditions that created the story's absence, a space which could not be filled by naming the speaker or supplying the author's intentions to a reader – could only be confirmed by a careful reading that did not deliberate over questions of legitimacy.

We would remain ill-suited for literature if we continued to dismiss critics because of what they did not enjoy reading: history that one could not predetermine for others. All writing desires the book instead of the moment, but not this book – until this moment is written. I had used history to learn for myself how I knew what I was hearing. Another answer that the theory of the novel gave to me while I wrote was the restlessness that turning pages expressed and had used to cause the book irreparable harm – perhaps the very harm that poetry would heal by letting pages, which were now filled with spaces, return to their original positions – so poetry was closer to nature than prose because it didn't ask the world to sacrifice itself to writing. "I have never known whether in discourse I should introduce my name as an intimacy, " I announced.

No one would listen to me because no one had heard me speak the truth – but this was a possible misreading on my part for the reason that words were less legible at this hour. I was already very nearly sleeping when I remembered the commitment that I had made by giving out the only copy of what I had spent no less than a fortnight attacking with work.

No other day but today had asked me to give this much of my time to accept such a small amount of sentiment from those who were not yet aware of me. Waking up was so difficult that I remained naked for an hour, and, by doing so, I changed myself because I had not seen my body in such a state as this before this.

Those distasteful pages were wrinkled with disuse and disaster. Because we were afraid we would forget to mention how full of exquisite tastes we were, we vigorously peddled their aesthetic positions all throughout the evening. I depended on clauses to see myself through each sentence on the way to fishing for an opinion. The page would soon be impossible for all.

Having difficulty sleeping led me to begin to roam, and I instantly happened upon my father finishing in the dining room, the television inaudible above the sound of the spoon scraping against his teeth. I wasn't seen, but I had seen everything. Childhood filled me with a continuous gravity that I cannot recover, although I have little nostalgia for a past made partially accessible. "The license tasted sweet to me," I replied, unaware of the indecipherable difference between permission and protection. Darkness didn't shine in on him. He was indistinguishable from the black background of the night into which I had entered.

We took turns, alternating between forms to keep the concerns fresh and distinct from each other, and produced the brilliant distance. "She wouldn't shine if I needed that from her," I thought; the lead snapped off sharply after I completed that pronoun with pride. The question of form imposed itself on me so strongly that it changed from being a game I played to relieve myself of all responsibility (a holdover from childhood) to being the strictest test to which I could apply the intellectual strides I had pushed myself to gain. Repeating the words did not mean I was having the same feelings again, but that the same words meant something new again, and I wanted to renew my commitment to them by saying them until I felt that I had no choice but to abandon them altogether for the sake of expression. Were we needed by the objects with which we had surrounded ourselves in order to flatten out and lessen the space between us and the walls, or did we fool ourselves into this line of reasoning to improve our abilities to closely read the various meanings of distances?

The one who had closed herself off to me was now having a wonderful time with the world, and, seeing her, it was clear that I had only made minor impressions; it would have been an inopportune time for me to yell out how old I now was. The man across the aisle approximated lighting a fire by jumping back from the door. She rose, crossed the room, returned to the corner, laid back down, pulled the blanket over her, and I was alone.

"At the moment I begin to think, I am covered in emotion." – this saying did not keep me from making lists of the few things that I knew were important to her. I had started to write history because

I was afraid what I couldn't write might say about my abilities to conduct myself, feeling the way I did about making words into gestures overshadowed by the significance of the context in which I had placed them. I needed less control over the past for form to push me beyond what I thought I knew I could say in sentences.

"For so long I have been speaking to reify my relationship to silence," I confessed to the class. And I was the poor professor who liked the power of standing before them, and I laughed at their every question. It was not this look that would silence me. As long as I was writing it after I had stopped thinking about it, writing that sentence felt autobiographical. Wearing the cap was the least of my concerns; I always renounce stupidity when I think with the force that those with unresolved arguments never expect me to have.

If prose is the form in which a writer attempts a novel, can a novel exist as a result of the force that turns history into a pure voice that speaks but does not tell?

Allegations would soon swoop down on him from the sky, as if from the horizon, as did the future, playing the role of a vulture. From the support I felt a sublime pressure whose originality made me more hopeful, almost optimistic. We had arrived on the scene too late to glimpse ontology as it polished off our vision; it could no longer speak for us, nor could it see what we saw. We were swept away by metaphysics when the question changed from poetry to prose, when I grew hungry enough to increase the words which hid the page behind and between grammatical blindness.

I quickly answered her question to keep the momentum from ending memory. I throbbed unlike any she had seen, conducting sound for no reason at all. She smiled and returned to the area where the pain had first been formed, a positive reinforcement for the power of self-control, as now she let me increase the volume and yell to empty my lungs into nothingness. Walking a grammatical tight-rope to test the multiplicitous strengths of sentences because of the faith I had in them as the smallest unit of writing I couldn't control, I wanted darkness to play an increasingly larger role in how I found repetition helpful to me when I spoke to the world.

No quicksand would have pulled him under the surface of earth because he had already resolved to remain hovering at a short distance above it; he needed not to put his feet on the ground, but to lift his head higher in the air and soar above the trees in a romantic splendor. I did not share, nor would I ever, these splendid and quarterly methods of timekeeping.

Rerouting the past pushed me to flush certain people out of its pocket. Football aroused an excitement in me too violent to ignore, and yet I couldn't overlook the number of players that had inflicted themselves on women and extended their theories of male aggression into the world around us, proving that art and life were wrapped together much too tightly for us not to take these contra-distinctions seriously as contradictions which compromised our abilities to speak soundly about the political means available to women as long as men dominated them with fists and bodies.

I learned that my greatest desire was speech, if only as desire. Finding it impossible to agree on a name, we refrained from addressing each other before launching our sentences, and anyone could read them and reply to them depending on the whims we would have aroused in them – but then they would flood these whims upon us. And is desire not something that ties us together at the thighs as tightly as this?

I have promised not to admit certain things to you – and now the door flies open, the sounds too loud – and my promises are as sincere as the things that interrupt me and interrogate the stance I have chosen as a means through which I can speak. "You are writing but not the silence of writing," I supposed. We will make plans together for the sake of keeping ourselves safe. I had come further in writing this than I had first imagined but had not yet written my contract because I felt fear when thinking thirty pages ahead – this fear teaches me the difference between the prose of a novel and the prose of a poem, as a novel is written to dispel the story whose unwritten existence causes the writer's fear, while each sentence added to the poem liberates it from the fear whose arrival is immanent, the fear that is yet to come. The horizon waited, it seemed, in the distance, and the sentence's certainty was written against the background of too many main events. My wherewithal was lost as I neared the end of my dictionary; this was too far from the historical moment to pick up and pose questions in regards to appropriating meaning, so it headed the sentence off at the pass that began it. I embarked upon no journey; I am waiting for novelty.

I had happened upon the wrong form, I had flown to the wrong country, for writing. The colors astounded, the backgrounds rising out of the scenes and joining the story I told of what I'd seen with what I hoped to see more of. Intending her journey as a thematic example, she showed me her penswomanship, smiling when I quizzed her about her intentions, and I slowly increased my awareness so I would include how letters were formed as roads across the page, which she had wanted for me to think of as the map of the universe we were building between us.

My eyes drained the silence from the room. It was in darkness that this solidity would fade into arbitrariness. "Don't force me to feel," I defended.

How dark it got in the room depended on what my father decided about the evening shining into the dining area, flinging the ending day in our laps, demanding that we recognize the horizon before we could no longer see it. I haven't yet thought of my mother, but now the sentence will trap her with my freedom.

Sustaining the ideas of prose are the material facts of paragraphs. I organize writing into ideas as blocks and bind history to the explication of each promise a paragraph makes. My thoughts have been sticking together in words that I haven't yet deciphered. The only promise I can imagine is the one that I will never reveal.

The boy who had not seen the fire did not climb the rock while we were watching. A light is at the edges of the door and the darkness holds fast against it when nothing progresses beyond it. We were fascinated in the restaurant, yet we hadn't even eaten. Were the pictures we had seen replications of a time that, if we had been given a chance to encounter it, we would have experienced as the original believers in destiny – or was this an interpretation that I repeatedly cited because it suited me for the appropriate distance in which I felt I had to clothe myself to control myself and become the kind of person I had once envisioned as a role model?

The rock seemed more solid, less lonely, without us around it, water surrounding the darkening ring.

It was through punching the pillow that I had attained such pure satisfaction, my anger subsiding, then seeping, through the wall. My neighbor was not the man that I thought lived beneath me; not only was I larger than him, but I hated him because of who he was to me in the past. Yet I had no recollection of him. I collected notes from the things that passed over me in the form of writing them down as objects I would one day appreciate.

She heaped our plates. I had cut these items lengthwise along the y-axis of stems that pointed the flowers at the sun, the stems which bent the flowers towards the horizon – not to question it, but to receive the promissory note of nature from it.

He vowed never to listen, to speak only when someone who was dependent on him was speaking to him, and, by interrupting them, he gained for himself the reputation of a man who had no time for explanations, for reasoning, or for insecurities, as these factors changed the nature of conversation altogether, asking him to play a significant role in shaping his responses and their resonance with his companion, when he was interested in nothing but silencing them while keeping them indebted to him. "Think of me as you ignore yourself." I spat at him again, my breath dissolving into smoke all over me again.

The man and boy both paused for a moment as the car raced ahead, missing a tree twice before finally hitting it, the boy's chest beginning to ache. I couldn't discredit this suggestion; I was its benefactor even when it did not serve the set of values I had grown into before settling on them. And then touching all the applicable bases sufficed to align me before the journey. I was pleased with this method of self-actualization. Was this psychology in its finest hour?

There was a slight hissing in the kitchen I would later rely on for reality. Typing this doesn't show you my difficulties with it or with my life decisions in relation to it. Leaning backwards and looking ahead of me typified the new movements I would have to make automatic, so I used a notebook to track my body daily in the hope I would soon transition rapidly from one side of the court to the other as I had seen on television. I would have to be ready for this night, regardless of my feelings for it, once ignited.

If the subject was prose, sentences did not answer for it, but for me when I wrote them and called myself a poet. Heat called out to me through my delirium. This she seconded by repeatedly pouring water. Then she was counting how much of it we had lost to the sun. Coloring in the liquid was a pleasure we would come to know through practice and steadying our nerves. "Your freewill is not independent of others," I ordered. I ordered my meal with style, grace, courtesy, and vision. Wary of what she had heard others say about him because of the things he'd supposedly done when no one was looking, she crossed to the other side of the street, and when she thought he was following her by flooding the pavement with light, she left the page entirely up to a host of historical determinations.

Philosophy had called – a voice, a silent cry, forever remaining in the air – and by answering it, they would have to recognize the pain responsible for this cry, a pain which asked them to empathize on a level their studies didn't anticipate, obliging them to seek greater truths than the questions their teachers had primed them to answer, and because the only dimension which authorized this voice to speak was time, they knew that the voice's impatience with their words increased with time – but they needed more time to sit and think before speaking for themselves and also becoming subjects.

I changed your name to suit you when I spoke to you about my relationship to authority, but I didn't authorize the errands to come out over the airwaves so loudly as to beckon us further along the horizon the evening showed us from a window. The thunder detached the air by answering the question negatively, accomplishing aphoristic truth, purifying the meaning I had hoped for.

We meant poetry when speaking of prose because of the functions we believed to be the truth of writing when we were actively performing it. When we were dormant it meant that we were due to speak more firmly about the preparations we were still making for the purpose of marking personal truth. "I have not seen, nor will ever I see, the other side," I predicted. Was the function of truth a mathematical supposition?

Wearing his face sort of softly, the man appeared to be shining for me and me only. A cliche had certainly beckoned me to listen to his sentiment, following it as closely as I possibly could with my ID flat out against the concrete. It was this man's voice that pulled me back from writing. I was a voice that belied the face from which it spoke, following what lay ahead of me, and also a way of possibly falling into it. I threw twenty years into a sentence when he laughed because you were better at projection than I.

The move did not shine down on us; it was clawing instead at the space in front of those who wished to look at it for entertainment. Art liquified the moment into pleasure. Life expectancy was a joke for the people whom we now think of as history when we laugh at their fictional foibles to strangely glorify ours. She agreed as to their humors. What they were worth she had not yet discovered because all the people whom she addressed turned to look at the sun when she punched the question mark.

I slung the words across the room, I mimicked the person who spoke in a manner I will soon inhabit. What I learned was that I could only become more like the part of myself I tried to hide when I hid it behind the others that I could never be. I speak for nothing so that everything might eventually write itself out for me.

As I entered, I was told that my leaving had been unexpected and in addition to the plan that I would have liked to extend beyond the sentence that promised it. The cup was always too hot; I am asked to pause and purse my lips before I pursue pleasure to its illogical ends. Consequently, having spoken without a logical aim in mind led to the fear of writing and the unsteady stalling that a lit cigarette acted out. So it was time to enter the other book; the first one did not seem easy enough for the application of my abandonment. My death was only an exaggeration when I spoke of it without concentrating on the effects this sentence had on the language I had always been speaking.

"I am less certain of repetition when I use the same words even more accurately." I was rambling and/or warbling. The interruption caused me to move less cautiously – I was permitted to leave more characters less complete in the hope of finishing them for the sake of ending it all for you as you also move. It's possible that I'm now overlooking all opposition. Another moment would have linked the instants with pluralities that may become collective.

Farther off in the distance than the man was the father, a retired keeper, who was reading a novel, turning pages too quickly for me to count them here. I could not argue for how far he had actually come. It was not the world around him that we could fault, for the world did not revolve around him; it ignored him in the same manner that it ignored any stranger who reciprocated its attitude towards the ever-expanding sky, and he sought the horizon, as he believed it higher than him.

I saw that they were in love, and they wrapped this feeling around each other like a blanket they were afraid they would forget if they were to neatly fold it and put it in the closet alongside other essential but unremarkable items that cluttered up their lives. They walked ahead in a line towards a destination I didn't see. The birds pushed, not thrust, their wings through a space I had never been able to occupy. To whom would I show this idea, and under what conditions would it be useful for those chosen to listen to it?

The body shook, with history's unsteady accompaniment, over the airwaves; this influenced my characters who began to parody their earlier movements by improvising the images these eerie parades impressed upon the screen. Suddenly the wheels stop as I listen for loudness to increase. "To drink it in is blatant when she needs to rest herself," I suggested into the microphone. "I will not submit to silence," I promised. But my eyes had already closed, had already been closed, before I could defend what I had been reading, what I would not maintain.

His writing and speech were markedly different from each other because of how he distanced himself when he spoke by fixing his eyes on the horizon, while, in writing, the horizon was the background against which I found myself reading his words. I did not find myself – I had already arrived and didn't need to be searched out. I found I was not ready to be stretched by that sort of facility.

Ducking her head solved the half of the problem she had been dreading for weeks, even years. This solution is one of many lonely worries. I turned and wrote to rough things up with language, which satisfied me under the conditions that words always apprehend from the world, seeking the end of things in the noise that erupts from their avoidance. I had learned that the question posed by the thoughtless – "What happens to a thing when we speak its name?" – assumed and asserted a fundamental division between words and things that we didn't see, namely because no level of history had ever broken the silence around a thing we had looked out at without formally addressing, and informally speaking to a thing was to assess it from a familiar position whose intimacy was not reciprocal.

But it was committing things to writing that I sought, a search to which I had arrived late since I'd been watching objects fail as reality pulled away from them.

More heat increased the need for the faces to die out. The boredom the looks on their faces revealed hid the reasoning behind it, burning the momentary sands that would always pass us as we gazed at everything we wouldn't all understand at once, crafting time as seen through a window. Having a reason for speaking didn't cause me to emanate or emerge through speech. "Are these what you wished?" I implored.

I carried form in my pockets, close to my thighs, in case my functions left me and lost me in the day. Its arrival had once seemed impossible but was now merely immanent. As long as I thought my way across philosophy, the land which I faced was fiction.

Actually, she had remembered the elements; she only forgot the various directions from which they would religiously return. We had photographs instead of memories and remembered the lone images whose negations of the sacred had become sheer repetition.

It flew past me. I chew slowly on these memorizations, small formations I make from the mist of hope, in the midst of home.

We sat forward to watch the argument at less of a distance than the one that had founded us in silence. It is only distance which interests me, stirring here because there are too many to whom I cannot be responsible by writing my way against time and losing it in the horizon of the day which advances and is still advancing. Prepositions do suppose the world, as it is only in the world that things relate by way of space, which is to mean that distance is an accomplishment of the world as seen in the way things are constructed – but because I hate objects, I spoke too quickly just then.

Here he will date me while everything near me ages ever evenly.

This thirst for words was all we could discuss; sublimating speech to sport was a mere mention. I was a part of speech as I mindfully became adjectival about all the daily events. Would such simple thinking limit things for us?

"Let verbal equipment lie beside you; put your head downwind and unwind what I haven't said" – I teased her in measured tones. Sadly, I digested the remainder of my argument, extending myself to appropriate the sense made by the advertisement this fiction brings forth because a poem will not fit the ocean if these are uncertain reflections of how people recycle distance. Yet my trauma was formed by what had made him so allergic. I was in a state of constant disbelief and would know no more of where he had come from.

Her short nursing period translated the months into a memory of what people once had done for each other with very little time to do it in. She agreed on the premises; objects in the environment obeyed her laws, yet the sun did not set against the events we had commissioned. To obey the ocean was not the horizon's sole objective. I listened to her shout his charming expletives and was later complimentary with my newfound commentary. Mishandling her words through misuse, she made me laugh unintentionally at language and not him. I decided not to take her out of the car; we started in on each other. It was good to be able in spots to do what we wanted. She slammed the book against the pack I had laid softly on the ground because she had money that she would always keep.

This poem is my way of not talking and of keeping my opinions beneath the surface of the world that forever erupts, a world which writing guesses at knowing by tackling it historically through unaccomplished sentences.

Time moved beyond us. Ruthlessly timing the waves, I put my arm into the sea with refined precision. The temperature gauged my level of attention; I looked across the surface and felt tense. No horizon would satisfy or poison her as she sat before this first fire. I always drag bags behind me while I walk, trailing them off into the sunset, becoming ever more distant by writing a characterization, not yet aware of the plot that is to shape me. But the flags that flew were interrupted by a solemn voice. Would this interpretation dismiss the guests?

Actually, we had just finished lunch and were getting ready for the action which had once alienated us and sealed us off indefinitely from the wind. It grew colder as time held us beneath the events I had hoped I could acknowledge by reading history, increasing my societal interest, asking myself more questions about how writing – a successive practice – taught us about what was around us and what I had thought did not touch me. Art did not kick the horizon; this drew me closer to it, distancing me from simpler grammar. But for me the trick was in being a do-gooder who didn't always wish the best for others out of circumstance, whose distant shifting often causes me to squint and think again. Would I be given more money for my tricks than the small amount over which I had heard them argue?

He carried the cart closer, perhaps too close to the sea, and I decided to remain silent about everything else. That they were always gathering around our spot when the man arrived disturbed me. This caused my writing to disengage itself from that thought and cling hopelessly to the more disruptive surroundings. If the parachute kept ascending against my wishes, I would have to close my eyes to experience distance, which tells me that I was perpetually attracted to the things outside of me, the things to which I am able to turn by writing, the things to which my writing has already turned. She looked down at the sand when these orders interrupted the day. Yet nothing could come between the sound of writing and the sea rushing in from the east. Where she wanted us to go charmed her because she had been convinced by what she'd seen that it was not beneath her, and since venturing had become illegal, we became severe by undergoing a well-versed change in attitude.

The day was soon made complete by writing. Speaking had always been difficult for me, but with everyone nearby surprising me the way they did, I was a fountain of illicit conversation. I, however, always spun words into phenomenological webs. Others often faced the wall. Happenstance certified every new hour. "I'm angry with the horizon," I unfurled. What type of speech invigorated such occasions?

But if a novel was what it was because it contained characters whose lives had ended for everyone in the world other than the reader, then to whom was the poem, based upon pronouns and what they didn't name at sentence level, directed when it was surely referencing people whose existence spoke to no one but the writer by refusing the pen's initial perusal?

I seldom spoke of my torpor. Many events had altered themselves by becoming unpleasant memories for me, tinting the windows to such an extent that nothing but the traumas I had faced, when I had drawn radically different faces, were visible. Enigmatically, I pressed on, using ellipses to mete out punishing phrases on no one, not even the evaporating air. Was the night as still as we had hoped, or was it the silence of the sky that so distressed me?

I needed writing to prove something to myself so I could fulfill the fortune I had gathered at the restaurant; I lay my hands to rest atop the unpaid bill. Looking through the glass door reminded me of the menagerie in a book packed with people, the shrill emotions of distant family members greeting each other in the middle of non-linear sentences. I held back my small, smack-dab sensations to make sense of the speech to which I felt responsible for an entire moment.

"Obviously, I heard the explosion, but I have yet to feel it" – the man had expelled himself from the occasion to summon stronger memories. Family had, only once, occurred to him as being important, and quite early in the first quarter at that. But it had always been in the shadow of the man that his father had been softly speaking, and these words rise and blind like dust in a vast field of difference. Never again would the air be the same air, as tragedy had etched its signature sentiment among him as he sat and spun sharp tongued yarns in a language he had never before been heard to use. Did he want me to touch him? Was that question a form of warning me?

It is the afternoon and the shop has been open since morning, although I have decided, with conviction, not to enter it and instead to concentrate on chasms, fluctuating along with splintering caricatures.

The intelligence of the conversation convinced me that few answers were legible. But by repeating what he had said to me, he made it clearer – but not completely clear (shattering the crystal only slightly) – that he had not said such a thing before; he had previously turned from me and towards the horizon to keep me from saying the important things that provided the vigorous reprieve I needed to relive. Luckily, I had been reading writers talking about writing, in which the subject seemed to be speaking as though it caused art to appear on the tip of the horizon.

She leafed through the photographs and looked for interruptions, distracted by her own telescopic drive. Phoning her author confirmed the mistakes she was to make. She didn't want to repeat them for others who wanted more from her than she could comfortably give in the stiff confines of one week. "My strength gives her strength," I would mumble. How could I have anticipated the heaviness in the only air we would ever know?

And yet her belief in heaven as a safe haven, a belief the rest were sure to immediately reject if she were to show it to them, allowed her to smoothly enter the conversation and change the terms on which she had silently agreed to speak. I wrote to assail her truth with profound images before it purely vanished. Profanities shouted from the passing cars avoided her ears altogether; they later arose when she spoke of the infant's lack of language. I grew silent about the infant. She waited for me in the back room to finish my goodbyes on the porch and return to her to separate my world view from her unwillingness to recognize it. Did I ask her to repeat these invectives softly back to us with conviction?

The fog slipped but did not dwindle when I called it back. Her sounds drew me away from the distance I had hoisted up onto the ledge of the room where I perched, shouting out through the doorway; I was railing against the evening as it was ascending, and I, through compromise, eschewed comprehension. But is the present so easily made, or made captive?

For this picture was a wonderful example of the futility of natural-
ism. It changed into pure light when it was beat too hard by light,
and the colors, which represent nature and push its faith in form
to a limit that does not exhaust it, chased the same resemblance to
the land's end, here where repetition reigned. I sat upright and
listened to nothing: my equilibrium slowly evolving and turning
with the restated themes, I learned the full extent of my lie. But
my mother's lie was not laid to rest by my return.

I balanced the light against my shoulder, the turning pages buzz-
ing (she was sleeping) in her ear, and faced both the opening of
the book and the open window. I was always more inaccurate than
the others were with my own open reading, but I was careful
enough to always have a book close by during inaccessible times.

I couldn't wait to return now that he had stopped slamming him-
self into what sounded like walls because of the emptiness con-
tained by the thuds. His melodies dissipated into disharmony. "It's
the noise of the nylon that I find annoying," I counseled. Surely
he would be asked to overlook his surliness by the creatures scur-
rying at his feet. He stopped all traffic; the distance from my desti-
nation extended out to a point in space that the map suggested
without making audible. I lit up the tree with lewd thinking that I
then made louder.

I write and later philosophize so as to anger the previously un-
privileged author who allegedly does not want to be read. Only by
being a victim am I now able to look at the boy whose father car-
ries magazines in his pocket, a man who imagines the current dis-
tance. The two of them giggled. And I would soon turn the handle
in against them. This closes in on me nightly with silence; I am
often meaningfully interrupted. I hoped what sounded like it was
flying above me would not turn out to be thunder.

It was a novel I had completed, for I no longer wrote it, but reading it back to myself generated an argument, telling me I hadn't written the characters that the book contained into existence, although I had never met them, which I attributed to the permeability of pure chance.

We were forced to alter the weekly itinerary. I misspelled the word I wanted to target and freed everything up into the purest sentences. Meanings around us asked that we unclench our fists. We cleaned our faces. It seemed to be nearly there, and my arousal was all I was able to confirm.

The misfortune on which we had capitalized was nonetheless rent with sadness in unsteadily unvarying degrees as an empathetic form of idealism. Of course, it was possible that the familial image we had so infused with sentimental value was the very item on the list in our hands we had found ourselves still unable to cross off.

My taste was as strong as she who agreed with me, whose mouth was as still as silence, but who did not shout this. Brightly she flashed her tenacity at me which was the cause of my unrepentant blush. Was it time for me to become louder than language with love?

The novel had been living quietly in my pack, dormant and denied the effect of criticism until my dissatisfaction at what the last reading provoked set off a sustained dialogue between myself and an unfinished product. Smoke unearthed the finality with which I was to spend myself this evening – through its minimal rise into the air, of course. My shoulders did not show the world what I had been carrying on them. My spine arched in the horizon's direction – but this did not reveal what I had been wishing for as anything more than a desire to exist as long as the future was more than a promise. And so I stepped forward even further.

·] 48

The father had set out to defeat his son with a lack of explanation. He would always learn everything he could about the predictions these peculiar connections had laid to rest in silence, leaving him beside the people we were likewise leaving. Such characters could not have been anyone he knew because he had let them all down. The music then acted behind him as a guide to preeminence.

I read the repetitions in her speech that rose up and assumed a fabulous form. She shrieked and instantly jumped backwards because she was a joke whose punchline I could not foresee, a surprise whose lack of humor humiliated her as she again thought of the horizon. Some of the dreams she had been sent started me off in an old direction, not steering me onto one I had come from. How would I know when what some had called good writing was too far from the time in which I was living to know what its requirements were, what those who had named it told me to give to the world when I was as autobiographical as a strange lark?

It was better than being alone as long as no one saw me doing what I was thinking. The tone behind his words was the reason that I had read him, but I could not take it with me when I closed the two covers; I was bringing them together as an invitation to forgetfulness and, sure enough, I had dissolved myself into another. We both excelled with a written lantern which uses letters to light the path of future progress. The things she had wanted to see me put before her were not the addenda requited by writing, since I suddenly remembered that I would have more time to develop my ideas because I was going to be given shorter blocks; this meant I could lead others through the thickest waters I had ever seen form a distance.

It seemed the novel was the surest way around the project of the Romantic Subject, which existed only in speech, because plot is defined as the action a story requires to be sure that it has taken place, whereas the speaker, as Romantic Subject, can only be sure to have taken place by speaking, assured that the story he is telling is being heard in its totalizing entirety. My father read such investigations no more. He snuffed out skeptical philosophy. Would such lights as these diminish my devilish projects?

Now I had no more wood with which to tell her the words that could not, in any form, attach me to a voice. "I am alert enough to hold him aloft," I urged. But after she walked out of the room in silence, I noticed that the sky behind me remained impassive, subjective, consoling: nothing else could have withstood such a dismissive display and passed up an attitude I later characterized as mature. Looking as if it were all that remained of time, nature planted its seeds in the humble ground before making itself accessible to the air. He emerged from nature with a small, potent scar.

An abyss at the very edge of expression was all I could tell her about what I hoped I would find when the morning was over; I meant to say that I was silent while walking into the room and opening the window with my hands. What she had been nodding her head towards was now coming at me; it landed with a thud on the sill. I began to speak slowly. I threaten her smile with the strange news by speaking too slowly. We courted one another for long hours over strong brews.

The conflicting reports hung us between them by putting our plans into question and destabilizing what was once a perfect day, petrified by time that had yet to pass over us as weather instantly chimed in. She stopped at each word and let it look lovingly back at her from whatever distance she felt it give her; I let the sentences corral me, but this is not to say that I let them touch me or my body, rather that they conferred outside of me and congealed beyond me if I were to coil myself around my thoughts of them. Actually, it was my father who sat over there and slapped the ancient screen with his aging fingers. I was to find this same advice once again in the interview I later read while disrobing. Were those the only words he did not slur?

"I will only ignore you when you yell at me" – I bargained with him for more unburdened time. Beneath us, silence proved that distance was founded on the most wordless theories we would find for ourselves; bold promises threatened the literature on which we had based our paragraphs as a reconciliation with a cinema that recorded objects without revealing them. We were capturing objects just long enough to forget the ways we found uses for them in the lives we were ready to structurally burst apart. But it seemed to us that it was a miracle when the words broke with the pattern established through pronouns, and yet the fact that the pronouns were what drove each sentence and made them become a force in opposition to history told us he was writing a novel because each sentence explained a facet of a character as pronounced by a pronoun. Length as a measure of expression promoted our story at faster intervals to the thinker. Philosophy ground him down until he was no more than a man standing before words as ideas in need of repetition. By downplaying my attempt at research that remained absolute in its lack of force, I became momentarily unbiased as to every opinion and thing.

She had deserted the apartment for the evening. I was thus left to read a writer who had avoided the act of writing by keeping up extensive correspondences, outlining a poetics of false aggression, abstinence crossing over into silence. Nouns, the rocks on which distances rested their sentences, were firm enough ground on which to stand and perceive the air that was always to precede speech, and that had forever proceeded out of it. She arrived home to find me staring at his penultimate pages.

I enforced more restrictions in writing longer sentences but did not cause them for the very reasons keeping me writing and holding words at bay with my autobiographies. I was similarly taken aback by the two globes. The new stain on the blanket took the day apart and then molded the solid shapes of future events, so we were able to rest while thinking of work we would for certain shun as hope crowded us out of our apartment. "I am my father's misunderstanding," I revealed.

She did not conceal herself behind ancient games when accurately speaking of history's rhythmic consumption. The hand that had stopped to pick up a pint worked no longer than the moment it took to move, a pen suspended miles above the page before becoming, once again, wet with wonder in performance. And yet I no longer thought such intricacies in ridiculing the sky over me that wanted nothing from me. The speakers exploded them as pronouns into space; an article I had read said more choices were needed in order to know what space was and how we could best listen to and use it.

My face, studded improperly with peaks, did not remain impassive because I had not traveled far enough to be described. To completely test this hypothesis is to turn speech into science. So many pronouns had become part of the tale I was writing that it seemed futile to ignore the whims of fiction to which I had long ago submitted, and the silence of the clock, with scrupulous abandon, adds up these empty names.

All ended as little for anyone but the distance in our mitts. If it were always to mist like this, we would have to remember the tarp every time and disregard our previous discardings. The candles burned. Someone would be waiting in the room beside me; I was left waiting and holding out my arms for all left unfinished as the future. I had wanted to title a book so extensively that the mention of its name would break open any conversation. The forces of conviction are now entering speech with the finality of a pen in the midst of darkness.

Increasing the spaces between the words was what allowed me to make the pages come alive even in the death that signalled writing. Repetition ended the dearth of words, being what constantly signalled meaning to the world as long as I am told to admit this as a form of knowledge – this is the magazine of thought to which I will renew my subscription. The way to avoid all prepositions is to keep from placing things in space, and yet this means that writing is a space we never manage to measure. I pulled on the lid to be absolutely sure of the level. Doing nothing for the rest of the morning revolved around everything I would still have to beg for. And yet, no one arose out of experience as a single, solid character that asked to be identified, making the experience one in which identification with the plot became circumspect, instead classifying an individual in time. The plot was a circumference I had drawn around the persons who had negated it.

Of course, it's possible that we were music, that the music we were hearing was what we were earlier speaking and had intended to eradicate. Later, I was asked to read a silent page as a promise; these sentences that flowed along the page's horizon did so not to save space, but to create the desire for it, piling my ambition atop the invisible flames initiated by books I am almost close to. Another book caused me to pause my movements because it revisited the question of fiction; it was asking me if lies could be sparingly told. Was it only in a poem that such scarcity grew tall without touching the towering distance of the sky turning me into writing?

For technology was not the concern that I had meant for it. The eyes which preserved the world around me had closed quite tightly. "My fatigue is in the way that I breathe," I reflected. If I were letting the light continue in its patterns, it was because I wanted to submerge the voice of the machine – a voice which hadn't displayed the accuracy that feeling, however fleeting, was leaving in space. I had hit it so that it climbed the wall ever higher; it forced me to run until the last man clapped loudly and laughed to describe the sudden victory, the silk silhouette of dying. Would she flee to protect what she saw die out so provocatively in me?

I had always checked to see what had been instantaneously historicized. When I found the same words in the exact orders that everyone had left them in, I became enamored of the vicious speed that reading uses to diminish its impeccable organization of themes. Time prepared itself to penetrate the projects I had laid out for myself. I seemed consecutive with my aims. I piled them up on the departmental floor. It was this form of distance I wanted to seek through repetition. We do not plagiarize the distant future in order to perpetuate the immediate past, however glowingly we have painted both in memory.

The title doubled up what I had written at the end of an otherwise original sentence, and everything else measured out the exact number of words that displayed the level of thought. No one word conveyed how words were held back to form dimension as in a bar of music. Depth did not speak for the essay on behalf of this diminished nature. And now I recalled the man with the piece of paper in his hand, a slip directing him towards the window and the water sliding behind it, to the left of the clouds gathering beyond the arc of the very word he could not pronounce because of the attachments he was too exhausted to explain the exigency of as a way to argue for art in opposition to information. As he walked with the hill on the side of the hand holding a cigarette, what the two conveyed more easily to the audience than each other was silenced by the drags he simply took. This sadness in their voices was partly responsible for an attitude I had decided arrived in the evening. Night was now assailable. "I lose direction when I fall too quickly," I described.

He saw no more shadows, reminding him of the time he was almost on fire and hid it from the boy returning water to the table at the woman's intimate request. My theoretical options became more oblivious to the historical facts because all the characters pointed in the same direction but not at the same vanishing objects, and, since my awareness was prior to my practice, to dismiss it was my way of associating language with losing control. The collective shouts without anger. The promise of finding myself at ease beckoned me into the room. I was reclining in a position I am ready to claim for myself after I see distance up close. The rumor from the north distinguished itself among everything else I had heard – not by its language but because I realized most desires in the final sentence.

It was time that I found an outline where constructing the next morning and afternoon made me speak gently with authority. In the next room, as the distance between herself and the past increases what she finds herself able to say, she listens to the consolations of stories that disembowel truth's previously precious and delicate systems. Time did not pass so easily as I had hoped, and the work to which I awoke was what I wished be part of the horizon no longer; I flipped over and then heard the game's soothing portrayals – here masculinity was highly priced. It is certain that what I have been writing, where I currently reside, imitates another book that I cannot have back from the world, even if that writing was given over to a noble effect.

The green notebook, which is not the only way towards writing, bristled longingly against language and asked to be discovered as the moment disengaged us from darkness. Breaking the pattern carefully enough to pick it up and examine it with the toughness of one able to resist what it argues, she held the object against her ear, accepting the agony more actively than my exemplifications. Autobiography breached the contract between the life that was lived and the one about which I had fantasized by suggesting the life we actually lead was more democratic through domestic lies.

I was willing enough to be an accompaniment, I cherished the occasion to summon the words of things to words I had formerly been apathetic, but to do this meant that I would have to sacrifice a certain kind of angle on living that allowed me to doubt life and enjoy myself. There are many lines left which will be used to line the page with words and thin the argument out enough to let you taste it, all because I believe art is a continuous change of taste in the place of infinitely paced plans.

The mail I was given governed what I thought of when I immediately opened it. Pronouncing my name correctly was not the same as summoning it – the look on her face told me this, eyes arched beneath the awnings of her anonymous approach. So small was the house that we felt known to each other while we were silently disengaged from, perhaps even disinterested in, each other's company. Had she offered me her distance to proclaim this silence as accuracy?

Intimacy between all members, including the boy who scaled the rock as we looked on despite our judgements, was superseded by the moment the door opened and the air outside sent the room skyward with impossibility. We spoke of how prose pushed us into our own rooms, the house filled with the clutter of writing because she had turned to pages as clusters of glittering ideas she allowed to tell her how thinking was only the energy predicting things before they materialized. And I stand with my legs hardly apart. Tomorrow is the plan she lays me in front of. We were almost able to close the door quietly behind us. We would continue to speak clearly into these faces. Now that the lights which I despise are on, reading becomes my enemy until meaning backs me down.

My fatigue, which I had hoped to shield from the sun, spent its time separating me from my work, and I labored against the mountain that desire had shoveled from the earth, an arrow serving as metaphoric vessel. When she reexamined the pamphlet, the pages I had spread across my legs came back to me in an instant of disconsolate recognition. I want to always return to repeat the experience of explaining how I know I have been living by deeds in words.

The sound at the edge of land bewildering the fact of space begrudged us his afterthoughts as he cleared his throat. I noticed the stains on his bottom row when I intended to smile, causing me to turn as I spoke the unrecognizable name to which thought reached out by molding speech into a character summary. "All intuitions initially respond with fists" – this is to say that movement is what I ask for as resolution, and an eternally revolutionary speaker begs my masses to sit down as the words invite them to question the meaning of work, violent assertions attuning them to passive effects. The political opinions I needed deserted me during the viewing – only history could invent the pure feeling that I called for in forming reasonable judgements. A voice from the next room was there to confirm the noise with broken glass.

The words made a kind of distance on the page we could not test with our own echoes. These dimensions outlasted the spaces we had so handsomely lived in, the comfort to which we had adhered as immobile as the invisible horizon we saw when we read on in our daily lives. And I hurt from what I saw while I read. The lights she left on for me were the objects I couldn't grasp without a significant shift in my adjucations; this was what the man on the stairs meant when smiling and sipping from his cup. I explained that I was not speaking of him to myself. The novel lay nearby. There were notable noises in the street hinting at a careful revalution of its surface.

The day about to end for me became the most specific reason for crossing the uncharted territory, banishing space into a position that characterizations often give to the underdogs who close in on wildness. Thus, the fans are now bewildered. She could feel these effects in terms of the temperature spreading unevenly across the outside. This suggested depth as an urgent message she did not wish to send back to strangers. She reinforced my managerial intuition. She turned actions into puns. I accepted her suggestion and agreed with the appointment, but not without a jealous tinge. I preferred to keep this anonymous; my job was soon secured as a figure who used the curtain to form language into a silence thrust into pillows of noise punching out pneumatic codes. Now that she fumbled with her index at the counter, letting the crowd know that she solicited their interest solely through her incompetence, I hung my head in the name of glory.

As I was at once alone again, I found time to attend to my aching body, a sign of my innocence, yet I lacked preparation in the end for his lack of control; my legs throbbed with impunity. We pulled our noses closer to the closest wall. We had thought history only existed as a backdrop on which our host had projected the horizon in order to catch the wind which sinks in the distance without naming the places it implicates. "I cannot fathom such copious copying," I exclaimed. But the weather was beckoning us to leave the house. Herein writing became necessary to link movement to the page's cycle through simple repetitions as a way of making the present an inaccessible example.

Her encouraging mouth moved, intentionally noticing me. Tension suspects the moments surrounding it with widening eyes in tune against the entrance.

Nothing I had heard him say to her betrayed the lies. Honesty happened at the very end of the screen, the car disappearing quite nicely for him. His attitude of entitlement filled her with filthy visions of people stripped down and chained in crowded rooms where the family ate together.

What I had last seen, but could neither express nor reveal, was how he wouldn't hide in the sand for the sake of our memories. I repeated myself. No more than one of the four was present during any of my revealing speeches. It was through speaking of the life I had put on hold that I could connect with it and forget the exhaustion of themes. The books hanging on the wall by the locked door remain silent and pious. I could sing my theoretical wishes to myself in the alley where I hid behind my imaginatively immune self-concept.

At this point, the central character has supplanted the space and time of the story and become only a voice out of which words flow, as in Beckett, but the confidence of the words that are spoken and the acknowledgement of a third party, whose silent interruptions are only assumed by the narrator, make the novel less an experiment in speech than a theory of what happens when writing becomes the subject of language and the author's idyllic narrative prowess does not prowl about the pages and prey on the reader. "I shape form from what I am made out of," I sniffed. And so went psychology, as such, on to further the narrative's dreamily subjective scrutiny.

I tried to return through innocence, which taught me to embrace fatigue and to exemplify boredom as it mutilated my capacity for humanistic feeling.

They wrote to forget what they say to me when they see me. Many kinds of men differ when it comes to choosing places at the table, but what this says, as I write it, is not to succumb to the pressure of taste, it is to turn taste into a text that is being easily consumed, unlike looking at and talking to the person with whom I count wayward mornings.

The patterns of his sentences lengthened as his letters grew more urgent about his need to wait and his involved explanations as to why he found it impossible to hold the devil's hand. He knew that his pen spoke out of his own sheer nocturnal selfishness. But was that only a filmic image, an impatient act of cinematic polarity?

As I now read him, I am thankful for the thing that lead him to his death and that allows me to complete my reading of these works in silence.

The total amount of description she supplied ultimately rendered adjectives meaningless because she loved them too much to speak through them. We recommended she leave only lists for us in order to experience a heavier, more organized bliss. For the world did not turn towards her. And as for cliches, she was disappointed by the effect of distance as a trivial effort. Sheer violence serviced her will to pleasure. This was defined through how the bodies deformed themselves onscreen. The subject of which I had been speaking contributed to my shame even though my smiles were never secretive. She left the light on for me for a sublime reason.

Soon the page will have pushed my pen into writing and over every quote outlining the duties of the artist to her work. The speakers feel they are artists only if they freeze their ultimatums which interviewers thaw out with heated questions regarding the nature of art. I was leaving holes between sentences; I could repeat my ideas with better, less pliable words that had come to define who I was to language in art. The best writing was that which I had yet to reap, only to read it beyond a long name on the otherwise absent screen, soon to be a landscape giving us an illusionary invitation to art. "Then I will only deify the horizon," I added. Yet I was in peril and compelled towards it.

Distance had escaped me and glued me to the world; this was the very thing that, as a man, I had been saving so I could one day give it to my children. I draped myself in his earnest misgivings. She was not part of the moment when I closed my eyes, but I knew, were I to begin the words, she would be ready to congratulate me, that occurring when I let my hands fall to my sides to say I was now silent. To repeat silence is not to duplicate it, nor does this version expose its weaknesses. It seemed as if pushing myself to achieve the crystallized distance of instructions exhausted my silenced sources. Soon waiting would take on the benign but mammoth presence of an action. And this immanence was discouraged by the lack of proper names I didn't know well enough to repeat in the message I felt it essential I send. It then became quite clear that nouns were the numbers by which I painted writing into my historical framework; the aches and pains these integers caused thus proved that persons, places, and things were what preoccupied language when it was also an object as well as a tunnel leading to the other half of the world.

What I wrote I denied because reading was less a presence than its exhaustion. We saw the sea through the holes in the concrete. "My fear is a form of arrogance," I would often boast, as grammar would become a vague, restless figure whose fate had strange, awkward, and restrictive effects on actions over which I cast my eyes. I saw across dim shapes. So I realized, while I was reading, that I had fused with his past; his energy erupted out of how nostalgia rubbed furiously up against the present and eventually coerced it, cornered it, and threatened it with spiritual harm. A project lying in the corner would suddenly wrap him in its pages and inspire him to reclaim this idle language through conversation. These holes were both illegible and difficult.

The time to teach argument had come to her; it was also time for her to quietly separate out its claims. I, however, found it unnecessary to subject myself to any forms of movement seriously considered to be action, as I was now in the throes of repeating what I hadn't done after all my reading on the infinitive. The open windows were unnecessarily evoking a week to which I did not want to commit in order to accept the impossible future. This was what they had meant by an underachievement when I heard them whisper psychoanalysis.

Cubes that became oblong as she closed her eyes also turned red easily into pale green as a simulation of aggregates. I had sealed the envelope. I remembered distant regrets in which agony was made somewhat untouchable by dismantling the mystery where I had hid them from nearly everything. I suddenly learned that this mystery was a pronoun in writing; sentences did not cause it to sing with the mercy I had convincingly encircled.

The line being rejected in favor of an original sentence would've held the hand of sentimentality so tightly that this prison will be what I later trace as the present source where we sound out our interiority by waiting.

Meaning, having become the sort of line described as a trickle, is the edge of everything I see straddling the distant line of the trees. It is the stories that tickle me. I was showing him the exact day on which the crisis landed – and he was new to this form of knowledge; this time the check would be blank and remain hidden from the family. We undermined our surprise with falsified memories. We had attached ourselves to the purity of change as a negligible, unwritten fantasy. I then thought to end as a means of preserving what I could see next and crystallize. When will I put my head above hers and so write? When will I put my head around what I mind, instead of what she's still explaining, and learn to wait?

The signature of autobiography is not democracy as the essay shows it to be, as the line of argument cut the notions of objects and their symbolic meanings into critical halves; if I say that these halves are organic, I have abandoned summarizing for interpretation. In time I polish my exquisite penmanship. "I am excited at this sole moment of silence," I decreed. But the return of the ants, their inhabitation of our intimate geographies, appeared in a novel arena, the bed we used as a couch. His response aimed the absence of its greeting at my pained insecurites in regards to the lack of furnishings. He found little evidence of this disparity and topped the claim off with sarcasm. Dust soon altered its form of containment, invoking comparisons with notably psychedelic descriptions of the natural world as a means towards psychology. Very few of the subjects I faced allowed inspiration to invite them home with me for the evening. This is to say that the duties I had been ascribed were falling back from me and into my space.

Prescribing light as a secret antidote to the remaining objects, distant through my inability to discern them, she likewise suggested I stay away from the purely novelistic. I consigned my father to a place in the sun in my head near the sea. All these methods are merely measures causing me to lean over the backs of the chairs which block our view of the spectacle; I need this promise and continue to push myself through it throughout. This is easily my most glaring accomplishment.

Autobiography's suspect nature permits a writer to narrate the moment in the first person while creating a separate moment to meet the pure lack of inspiration, the scene only as close as the last general relation – which she'd noted to herself – between her ideas and the pen between her fingers. Paying a debt to romantic theory, she criticized the present's inability to put aside the past for the sake of an innovation she would later provide by quitting theory in all of her writing except personal passages that critics had divided from context and altogether decapitated. I felt delightfully shameless about this reasoning.

This was the kind of job others had cautioned me against taking. I now understood their wanings. Every tree is innocent of the knowledge of me, for as I am writing them down, objects become less signified in the words that own them. Objects are in the employ of these words and are obfuscated by cautionary measures. My perception is itself an object within its own limits.

When had the toxicity been driven into him with such force that one piece of it suggested another by overlaying the second atop the first?

It is clear that the purpose of repetition is to reinforce controls and contexts committing him to the subject of reining in meanings from the landscape and surroundings. All such writing would

·] 68

reach the level of noise when the sentences became apparent to the owner, clever patterns stating the world that had been totally staked out but still unthought.

I cheekily mentioned our feelings for our comparative oasis as a way to lock down the quiet destination in the distance and make it essential reading. This message would lift her cleanly out of the box. I suggest that looking at the world whose purpose is to push us into the day, beyond the day whose sense we inhale, will allow the leisure to let us lie.

Agonizing in such a brittle manner, touching arm to thigh – all pronounced the movements as purely in the moment, punctuated by oblivious, obligated immediacy. The two men tied themselves together for the sake of forming three legs; a fourth exposed itself when the woman decided to apply polish and remove the skeletal framework looking like an invisible cage to the few of us in atten-dance as the audience. Repetition set the standard in time as stone and mediated between the perceived gift and the received quo-tient, the act penetrating the sound as only as the day would per-mit. But everything was not arranged into master and slave. Labor tamed the morning; it was teeming against the frame around him; because of this pressure, I ardently declined openness.

I silently ignored the credentials, in spite of their noteworthy no-bility. Would it have had such language if this were a novel, and so much more of it?

But now convinced that I could take writing with me anywhere I went, my notebook turned mysteriously luminous, confirming her numerous theories regarding art's essential ambiguity. "The crux of being lies between us," I implored. She had dug no further than the past, which we can only approximate through calling it a wound. Oddly enough, others also let this nomination fall recently from their lips. Adverbs keyed in the meanings of my actions through stating the methods I used to handle objects, and the novel that avoided them resolved to dismiss actions from the object so as not to allow them their pure permanence.

I suddenly remembered a lyric because of my passion, only to be struck by its elegant stronghold on the present. Each time I entered the gates of the present, I would be hit in the face by anxiety; I carted new feelings around with me in a display of time's organic dissent.

We were now unmoored from our complete mastery of the areas on display. Our wizardry was such that we arrived late and seldom practiced while answering the questions with a cheerful, nearly relaxed, lucidity. Towards which day would we target our actions? Why not the next one to prove the virtuosity of our following?

Clipping the wings of my feelings was the easiest way I knew to have a patience I could casually mention. I found when I wrote the letter there was more to add if I included the cover; this inclusion pointed towards an identification I had previously sworn off because I did not edify it in my romance with the intellect. But my sentences seem to be patterned on the struggle for communication that stretches the bands of teleology through the assumption that what is said last is remembered first by the listener; all who listen make a list of what has been said, beginning with the inflection extending into silence and backtracking until the final repetition is the silence out of which speech bursts onto the scene. This sentence is circling until the place where it ends is at the center of community, where neither speech nor silence are inaudible.

The crouch of the man in the aisle could have been easily applied to the type of stance that prepared aggression for the purpose of winning back what another threatened. His fame was an affair puzzling me; I identified the pieces I read as melodramatic biographical fragments I wanted to twist into memorials. But no cramps would tie me down with their tightness. His favorite album on the turntable, his funeral turned fame into famine – I was devoured by these simplicities because of his devotion to others through events. An arm lifts the very substance that will become indistinguishable from support, like the way a word, at once an effort of heated abstraction, nestles comfortably into the flow of the narrative, only to rest near its back exit.

My sleep was often interrupted by worry. A compliment helped me to feel helpless regarding my influence, as though I was not against the wall, and I remembered particularities emerging from what I could no longer call nowhere, as I have never been there and still look to language, which retrieves it from the distance.

All morning, I found the obsession with the biography a matter that added to the increasing anxiety of the following day; I did not leave my own life behind by reading it. Likewise, every horizon she sees appears to her as the most perfect form of repetition but does not suggest a replacement. I wanted to write in the way of silence without giving space to it. I am ultimately intending for silence to emerge from everything the words I give off grasp. I replicate the day replete with inequalities because I do not see so evenly, nor do I cast my eyes across the space before me; I survey it only when I think of it no more.

Now she sits outside on the chair with a smallish notebook. Its pages are safely rounded at the corners. She whispers, "Surely a story based on the uncertainty of pronouns," (these did not follow the subjects she nicknamed but preceded them), "says that familiarity breeds the formality of addressing the unknown with careful trepidation."

As they danced, a third man cut in and stared at the first to push him back with the things the first had second-handedly heard. I, too, had weighed the prohibitions of proper attire, learning the limit before I broke it, and I decided that these formal concerns were the very addenda that, after I edited them during construction, would allow my creativity to reply so thoroughly to the blankness in my notebook. She listened to what she had had to say to me by rewinding the tape, my voice rising to divide her concerns among afternoon hours. And the roofs, with their thick slabs of metal gutters, introduced us to buildings we assumed were infallible; we began to step up to meet danger and remained on the outside of art, but she didn't dare move after I tore up the daily pages.

Synthesized sounds had been recombined to form new entities whose aural properties were more akin to wind than music; the booklet exclaimed that the dividing line between nature and production had erased itself long ago. Our attraction to what we were hearing was based less on our recognition of nature than our wonder at hearing its insurgence turn active through manipulation. "I am an advertisement, no longer" I said, sounding coy without being so.

The wind boxed us in our building because it blew in from all sides, so we began to open the newspaper without letting its noisome rustling affect us. I felt tired. My voice was too weak to meet the required level. Yet I had to accept the oral demands of my profession. Now I see how hard edged the pages are that beat back against us but do not bear the traces of the wind.

The words could let the characters eat up many pages – but not assign this task to language; the fact that none of the characters had neither names nor goals in the narrative was proof that, while this bit of writing did not pay attention to individual words, it abandoned its characters to the sentences that claimed them, and, by doing so, yielded them to grammar.

I had forgotten description so that I might survive – until I read a line.

Until I read a line as an indeterminate sentence, they would never undermine the work I had examined so solemnly and later let go of for the proof of prosperity. I let the houses become more brightly lit than the language draped across the sequential pages. The presence of greater visibility showed me the willingness to hear the noise cast off by others' bodies in the wake of pleasure. I am ready to present the material I do not know to the extent that I am able to speak of it while thinking of something else that does not relate to it. I find that the material resists the things I would impose upon it for the sake of my own intended pleasure, an intensity I would have nevertheless continued had I been told how impossible I would find it to apply it to what is reasonable.

Diversions didn't mean that there were two subjects. The object left one behind in a false pursuit of the other, where chance glittered on the horizon, lingering long enough to attract. Negativity guided us. We were then wary of what it meant to open our mouths and receive no food. Why did I find that repetition could be decided upon with the most figurative actions, like tying a shoe and later throwing a stone to catch up with myself?

She drew back from the wind. He left his bed in order that he write with his eyes against the distance he doubted was caused by the view, with the ability to notice he didn't create it. Even as the day was still dark, we found our need for the darker substance, to drink it in for the words we had used in silence.

·] 74

Noting that so little time had indeed passed was not an indication of more time: the day was less than two hours from ending and less than six from when he would have to rise again and work. He found that the past, a subject I had used all my energy to avoid, was the item that drained his own energy, as avoidance is more tiring than the aftermath of acceptance; this acceptance formally invigorates the speaking object with a feeling that does not flow into malleable territory in order that it be manipulated. I heard their laughter on the stair tell him the neighborhood was uneasy. He thought he might see me again and turned his head to the phone and the wall that held it up. Later he would remove it from the wall in an act imitative of another's masochistic imagination. Yet that was the very sky he didn't want to hang over him.

The novel was secure enough to contain all of its characters in its pronouns, while the poem might repeat the same pronoun in five consecutive sentences and mean different characters or mean no one but that pronoun's secret identity the narrative folds neatly into itself.

I longed for more time because I had had so little of it when I was young – not because I was busy, but because I was always being watched, so that when I was idle, I was made to feel nervous about my lack of production. Yet I had nothing to produce because I had nowhere in which to produce it – except for my imagination. "I often twitch when I feel controlled," I offered. This was another repetition I had unearthed, my cheeks reddening with sudden remembrances.

She questioned the certainty of the clarity of the images – their colors recommended connections to the world in which I had grown old enough to become active in my disillusionment, but this is not to say that I had successfully turned my life into a novel, as I would still have to find ways to put sentences in the mouths of such characters I would forever seek to unfurl.

The connection did not allow for enough honesty to expose the overflow of my timed boundaries. I sought a lengthy acknowledgement, I sent a message and requested a change in the truth value of the question I was going to be asked. I would finally relax as I presented her my material; I was only responsible for all of its meaning. But my fatigue prevented this from happening.

Even if my fatigue prevented it, I was indebted to writing, show-
ing this by staying home and plowing through the once smooth
fields of pages for half an hour. The short sentences seemed to me
to be what to her were the most important things to say without
fully unloading meanings into the discarded pile of non-reusable
cartridges. But she would read about evidence soon enough. Of
course, this was harmless dischord, but it was not harm that wor-
ried her – she'd found herself fully armed with danger – it was
rather the intent of the ink marking up the page without giving
thought to ambient sound, cool clumps of impressionistic, vesti-
gial greenery. I wrote at the very moment she read aloud to others.
Counting pictures on the wall told me I'd seen much less of the
world than the lectures I'd ingested. But could she know how loud
it was for me in my room lined with too many windows for si-
lences to belong to this space?

We did not watch closely enough to see this space together.

We spoke eagerly of how the paragraphs were organized along the
same lines as reptiles and the sizes of heads and claws relative to
torsos. This wasn't the same as fucking, not that such a desire
presented itself, but something physical ebbed and flowed in tan-
dem with these floors, liquid enough to be limply presumed as
thirst. I like rhyme to defend itself; it defers the moment in which
closure arrives. But being alive only happened during writing be-
cause then thought no longer filtered its way through the many
restrictions also called flaming hoops. "I am used up by the noise,"
I conferred. Then an interesting slogan of interrogation slid its

repetitions into the air. Remaining blank by association, the line will seem to ask for writing while it nonetheless serves as a reminder of the job which draws me back into further climates.

I am ever distant if the past is a microcosm of where my life is presently headed. She heeds grammatical fireworks as an offering of intentionality. Both of these ideas bracket work if thought is the subject. But was it possible to write a novel in such a way that innovation in terms of character bypasses the era of novelty en route to the polar extreme of art as a social structure?

Twenty minutes, the twin of the ten made solid in a promise, took away the time of transcribing from the journal serving time in a notebook as a novel. She wrote of her job. Employment provided her with an opportunity to professionally grow and tell others to smile as widely as she had when taming her superior. She did not offer him her sexuality. She knew little of the troubles that arose before he came – these troubles for which, because she is now where they first arrived, I hold him partly responsible. I shall keep this invisible. I will permit him certain trespasses to watch him nod his head so excitedly. For such extravagance rarely shows itself. And yet another working man who looked at the chalk marks is vivid, as his reasoning causes them to laugh while he's drawing over his initial marks. This cancels them out through repetition.

The world in which psychology was master was the very world to which she had dedicated herself, prolonging my ignorance and suffering me all the more, for I soon found myself banished to this same ignorance because my anger had formed an impenetrable forcefield of resistance around the entryway. Now, as I am shouting but saying nothing, I realize that reality is conserved by the front door I must forever enter. Would I accept the writings I brought back from my physiological travels?

The pictures he sent us turned us on to the fact that his dementia was exposed to us when he visited; we thanked each other for the vigilance we had each shown with our collective answer when he asked us if he could use our couch as an eternal launching pad. My attention was everything in relation to my needs and thus subordinate to the shoes I was destined to fill and to proudly wear out. I recalled the sentence in which he had exposed us to everything we should have worshipped of the subject causing us to gather; I would later be doubtful as to this meaning, being dutiful. He retained the remainder of an unlikely consciousness containing the distant meadow. Had the signs he flashed meant little else than the violence displayed by emptiness?

We will always disentangle ourselves for more fun. Exhibiting such overwhelming emotion that we were unable to follow the preordained speech pattern whose agreement arranged the audience's expectations, demagogues to the common men and women who'd set aside their afternoons for glorification, we nonetheless succumbed to chaos without ever becoming truly impotent. Was it possible for my needs to obliterate this infancy, this obstinate moment which did not tick but purred with the purity of a machine while I wrote with apish determination?

All sound was soon a song not yet hung in tones. I had divided the day up into simple, simulated fragments. Now it would be known – the nature of repetition was such that opportunity prevailed by becoming less precise; thus the effect was left to recite what was cherished in deed.

The door, jarred into action by a firm wind, kicked his attempt in that afternoon, but he would now pick it up again, having reached the forty-minute mark, a time seemingly grounded in the everyday experience he had set aside to listen.

The three painful days made it possible I could then have the rest of the week to try and fully awaken beyond the level of gentle, helpful comments aimed solely at reducing fault and piercing a hole in despair. Could a crisis count as the kind of interruption which qualified unconditionally as love?

He spoke with the sort of passion that I, a listener, usually expect from someone making an altogether obvious confession, and although the words the rooms were to receive were not autobiographical, I could hear them in no other fashion. But could inventing sentences neither connected to nor comforted by the others surrounding them be the answer to the problem of context if context, while perceiving the difference between ideas for the sake of democratic idealism, spread us out across the fields of interest as a quick decision to either accept or decline each other?

When she announced what she would wear, the price of the bar-
gain ballooned unreasonably, and the traders exchanged unwit-
ting glances with the bartender, hoping his words would change
the talking fabric. And yet the image of a rock mistakenly pro-
vided the meaning he'd intended. Later, she threw herself ahead
of him to invite in the possibility of future headings for the gun-
slingers. That last word, in its singular form, was the title from
which I had yet again stolen the two of them.

Hiding in the front seat was a method of avoidance I had used
mainly as a means at work towards indefinitely ending it. My voice
reached the end of the room and swayed them into silence; it lacked
topical immunity. All of her efforts at speaking of art rendered paint-
ing mute, an unimagined figure that would never appear. The
figures moved in a strange manner; the new spectators thought
the goal was to refute the argument of grace we had come to see.
We had written pages on aesthetics that added up to piles of wor-
thy musings on the imprecise nature of tastes overwhelming the
margins in which they had been previously contained. And social
control was a gesture no greater than waving one's fist in the cur-
rent air.

The coin which I turned to for chance never mirrored all that for
which I had been lying in wait, and, when I sat on the step, I also
sat at the feet of my repetitive actions – because I needed to walk
and to shop as I hopped towards fate. Soon enough, I would be
returned to my angular convulsions, all arising in the absence of a
face to connect his voice. Hanging against the wall is the very ob-

ject I must always evade so that I may never know what it is I am working for.

I required, desperation in hand, that he be ready for the moments when they would sit and wait for the organizations to drop on top of them, but the kind of preparations I would have had to accept clashed with my innate sense of spatial relativity.

Evolution precipitated dingy reasons for the application of adjectives to static, expensive nouns. I asked them to answer for grammar. They asked that I speak of his grand mal, baiting me with the silence typified by all back rooms. I had come to correctly perceive and so name my apprenticeship because of this silence.

She piqued only her own interest, and only because she learned that her need for reason overshadowed the structures that it legitimized. Not remembering the number meant that pointing wasn't preliminary. She screamed in such a way that he distorted it in such a way that the words he was speaking retreated from the playing field where I had been listening to them make meaning. "I am at full capacity now," I muttered memorably.

My twitching eye repeated memories that, I was told, were not a psychological symptom, but an outlet for that symptom, a place where my body could rest its movements and visibly express itself. And we know the way these roads circle a barrier will always remain only partly visible; it is also known that it is the roads that need to be focused on. Is the novel less gentle than this poem? Is that because we know which character is supposedly being engaging, the journey that is actively being suppressed?

But he supposed he could always work each day because there was too much left undone in the way of saying things about events.

Those going to arrive throughout the week could not have known that he wanted to have an ear listening to what he was still seeing posted outside the office.

The subdued and ordinate interest in the theory of the absurd, a sentence that fingerprinted and purposefully reordered itself, left me with the feeling that I was still too far from the day hanging on my door. I did not hesitate to hold back my explanation of those items that lead to conservation. I had awoken early. Her greeting provided smiles in the car which was to otherwise stay silent, where I could pretend to think and read on ominously when the speed increased to meet a deadline full of undefined resections. Would waiting be the activity through which I would start to remain, however long it took to learn those rules?

Neglecting the rules, a type of rebellion on their part and a type of resilience on my father's, made for investigative moments of recall, but those times were barriers to the kinds of commodities I searched out; I soon found myself composing succinct preludes. All those names created anger with the silent excitement each banner replicated for me. Banter escaped into the room around me. And was it also so with wings that did not sink into sand as I was watching them from the falling air, falling as I rose up into this with trepidation?

She was keeping her silence to herself so as to be sharing only her noise with me as I crouched and pushed past all we hang loosely in the air for inspiration. Autobiography informed me that novels were the major methodology predestined to rage upon crowds. "I am filled with your false faith," I confessed. We began to make plans for the day when she would be the sole provider, when I could dawdle in the dangle of less eager language setting me up now that I sat on the outer half of time.

This was the record I wanted, and I accepted the melodrama saturating the room. Every time I stood at front of the room I was battling for control even though they had to pass by me to achieve life consciousness and the apex to which it was affixed. But this consciousness would go unrecognized by others who did not know them if they did not write up their own desperate connections and scattered their faithless remains over the immune and immovable sea.

The binder protected the crumpled pages that would have been otherwise torn up on this enforced occasion. But it was only for twenty minutes. Words fought through the bindings and restored pathologies to the origins – all were methods of avoiding unresolvable pain. This technique did not become metaphysics as the philosopher had once so confidently been quoted as saying by the teacher, who told them "become explosive by writing esoteric quotations." The time hadn't yet arrived. It nevertheless slipped out of the seat and into a crack beside the door while the trees let the sun defeat what remained of their no longer avid growth.

I was a novelist, but the composition requirements would surely have shown me as the one who was giving my sentences' instructions short shrift. Cliches falling from the sky let the air become new for me with the disengagement from meaning; but she next said that "meaning is as impure as chalk marks." Would the man know that I was capturing fugitive words I hoped to someday find myself in the employ of?

He would wait near the open door.

She will later inhabit the apartment, unlike the close fiction the radio is forever reporting. The room turned into noise. Here the first day, a seventh repetition, found her newly nervous about the impending crowd no longer in the distance.

I speak again of fatigue, as it has not left me. Anyone we see could say this just as easily as me. All the rates of conversion did not converge with the goals I had immediately set for myself; I likewise found my failures to be oft repeated as a result of that which riveted me to the past's preliminary philosophic hierarchies. The rain affected the day, its immense programming outweighing chance, but my mirror was thickly coated with the immunity of chance.

I disliked the time I was given – it was hardly the refuge from work I requested, and I filled in the cracks with my worry; I built a compound sure to hold up in and all throughout time.

I'd wanted to read this kind of book, so I made sure not to write it when I was feeling that silence was the reality of all the language they were allowing me to use. Modifications, methodologies of thought as it distances thinker from subject, were what I subjected myself to. And I sit against the invisible window. These cramped lines will serve the immediacy of accepting the page that ends by beaming down on the dreams filling another misleading notebook in my life.

Clouds had become the crows I filtered the sky through as crowds. But in two weeks I would know what the observer thought about such radical reconfigurations, for it needed to fix itself on the wall for them to then chase it down. Would I return to my writhing promptly enough for the exact difference between the sentences to show and be seen?

She sat on the couch and explained the theories to he who was also a composer of some renown; the slice balanced curiously on his knees, he rocked comfortably backwards. It would be much later when he was finally able to reach the door with composure. She saw how long it took his anger to subside in books. He had buried himself beneath a pile of discs, carefully labeling the undecorated covers himself with typewritten ink. She wrote fondly of me, as if to say we were each other's happy companion in the past, but only I knew that, if asked, she wouldn't return to the terrifying scene in the basement. I protected her by forgetting. I thought my methods through all that stayed at the level of the senses.

His memories were like mimeographs of blurred discomfort, copies anyone would have wanted to throw away if given as a familial example. I praised him when I told him it was his insight into the nature of the psychology of the witness that let me think it. Later that evening I feel my shoulders tighten up. He spoke of what drove him back once again to seek support in a slow voice.

Now it is the doors that close. Time polarized all things with evaluations. But this did not mean that I had them. The memories I decided to accept were those I was in the process of erasing to eliminate their sharp corners.

She felt that leaving a notebook near the bed was as close as she could possibly get to dreaming in sentences translated into perfectly readable writing. I stayed home; I read the kinds of books I wish weren't written so as to mine a particularly painful depth, throughout which I feel the pure confusion of hitting a horizontal wall. Some body parts needed more protection for the protagonist than others; and yet when I lay in bed my hands sought only one to save because of how small and sad it seemed to me, even in the dark, when it slipped unnoticeably into an invisibility seen more clearly in the window.

They were speaking my name, of my lack of prohibitive movements. Then there was the day I stood against the locker and breathed because I knew I wouldn't be able to speak for years to come. Admitting the truth brought me less relief than pretending there was no such thing, so I kept silent and wore a half-smirk. I want to talk about this with these people. But they all stare weakly at me. And I remember the locker now. Would ten turn to eleven if the weeks didn't continue to count by not moving towards an inescapable examination?

"He is the master of declaring the meanings of sentences," I quipped. I go so slow as to allow the pen to limber up and grow erect, but I do not come when being looked at by the words that leave me. The image was of a large body splayed out over a smaller one, kissing the face and holding the nether parts without stroking them; the small body felt itself in limbo instead of liberation. And no narrative diatribe had found me as gloriously as that long distance call placed on the horizon by a message that repeatedly wanted me to receive it with thorough, yet placid, patience. Could it be true that so many read this section on this very day, and, if so, what did this tell me about the many possible divergences among so much more role-playing?

I needed to see her more closely so that I could begin my weightless ascension into questions. Yet the book with the wordy cover and worthy self-help exaltations was no further away than the remarkably colorful but slow loading screen. She cannot move as quickly as the inferences allowing me to count up who this we is that is repeatedly annulled in the torrent of words.

These handwritten caresses become accessible to the many men in me whose palms are stained with mail and bruised with milk. And they would soon close up.

I had to hurry to gain secretive access, an inviting theoretical endpoint to a poetics of ridiculously formal inclusion. My fingers danced in a circle of inevitably wrong keys while impotence filled my precious journals and dreams because of the graduate assistant lackey I wanted to become a treasured object for and escape my psychological fait accompli. But the absence of characterization, regardless of the weight it forever carried, did not mean I hadn't been autobiographical, as the blank truth of the words was that they were not yet subject to the poetic condition, a consciousness wherein meaning lay between the sheets, bedding down with both writer and reader in an involved act of fully clothed foreplay. Blips and squeaks lectured us in leaks and slips, converging in that veritable movement of the only author possible for philosophy.

Then they allowed his wooden speech and leaden tongue to loll into unnoticeable avenues of discussion. As soon as he arrives, it will be obvious as to the quality of this obsession and its effects on the remaining weeks before they do not ask me to return, the outcome of that which I am ever so sure and so follow. The valiant efforts of all were what I kept in mind when they spoke to me of him before the open gates in husky, honeyed tones meant to hinder my pattern of indentifying with kindred spirits.

This is the professional disbursement I confess to the stars.

A few smells do not leave the living room for days. I am always hungry when I write here after she eats.

A shirt showed the magazine's transpiration. Arriving early enough, once again alone, filled with nothing but anticipation, my nerves soothed by the tape because it was surely a greater truth than the mouthed words – this was what I would otherwise call waiting. Was the sentence in the wrong place or had the student fit it in the only slot available to her in which to think?

Droning along with the fitting end of the evening, the student punctured the windows with that synthesized, sympathetic laughter out of which the devil, the king stooge, is what we make out to be as metallic. But he was always bellowing, his voice an absent echo as his lip was pushing back through paper. Over one half hour, he didn't bang his editions into those who were waiting for the messengers to neatly congeal and cling to the walls.

The seriality of things made way for consumption, unlike the act of ducking that the survivor told us was the perfected familial image of a masked urge. I concluded that shortening everything can reverse the coin's dissatisfied face. Water runs along a nearby path, close enough for an earlier proposition to seem downright eerie, while philosophy drags us up against the threshold of language, and we gasp and gape as we glimpse these inner limits and the goo to which they stick.

Flipping through for the answer he'd wished, after finding it, he'd never searched for let him know he'd entered the wrong world, one which he'd been warned against while reading those fantasies written by a fanatic. The writing wanted to break with grammar and go against the prescriptive grain. Newer experts acted with increasing snobbery. Her manner toward the figure holding his head down was as unfaithful as the heroine crossing the pathos of deservingly delirious men. Then another brief poetic device entered the field of play. And little could explicate her fascination for him, as she was blond enough for him to wish he'd been blind to his own penchant for pursuing unwanted, necessary, pain for personal growth. I conclude that the passive voice just might be the appropriate tone for writing to use to turn to observation while still filing the language away as value.

Having neglected my own interpretations, I swam into a kind of light the distance culls and immediately crosses with its straight edge. This is then to say I knew the way my own unfettered desires would forever look to others as they peaked on the horizon. This invitation was another kind of interpretation – much more formal, one requiring its recipient to dress herself up in the motif of inaccessibility.

She tailed the lead for a chance at staying with its riveting light. But would the ones who eventually read the cover be able to see the clear lines the writer had drawn between the priority given to stylistic poses and the means towards preserving the piety of instructions?

Exhaustion caused me to chase after the paralyzing parataxis; I hunted until she was the last vestige of deixis left standing on the printed page primed to be read in permanent silence. She is sleeping in such a way that I have thought of her always softly, always as a place for me to go and relive a once uncomforted anxiety; she reverses these effects.

And then they surrounded us, so we debated the virtues of carrying houses on our backs versus having the furthest reaches of the earth ringing in our ears.

He wanted to force the walls to shake as an expression of his deafening depression; he defended everything with his gold and glitter coated platforms. Few films have mined reality for fiction in such a heathen manner of sloth as this, extensive directions that pull the viewers back towards the couch – even beneath the cushions where the crumbs slip away and become temperamental memorials to a dying cinema. The heavenly manna I chewed earlier is letting me begin this so close to stardom. The afternoon was accomplished in a single act of negation, as I was on the eve of a technological demonstration on the latest path to stardom.

No longer would we find ourselves having to follow directions for which we had only negative feelings, and yet the majority lamented the structural loss of this world they could easily hate because it belonged to anonymous crosses. I divulged, hoping they'd accept me instead. As the evening found its way to her from across the horizon, she, too, drove back with a clear vision of what they expected from her work. The bird that chirps to avoid boredom, cheated out of its colorful freedom, singles out the most important aspect of this wind, a windfall I keep to myself for the sake of saving secrets and feeding on their pressure. Then we read historically on.

I liked her looks just enough to exclude her from the tyrannic fantasy. And so the dogs that howled behind me did not give chase. All that seems historically fruitful is also grist for the current mile throughout which I continue to disengage the machinations of narrative describing this very page, one I feel close enough to to imagine I have already signed it. Absence flees this imponderable scene even as too many words are filing themselves behind the cabinet where I study the act of writing by practicing it as do frantic people.

I abruptly stopped when he hit the city's exhaustive limits yet stooped to avoid the door coming to a rapid close. I could not read such a small book slowly. Now I begin to nibble at the cover's corner, the taste unlike the drink I decided was too thick to nimbly follow what I held (unsaid) in my mouth.

·] 94

Scenery, awaiting our invested intensity, fluttered beneath the bat-
tered girl who would be ready to take us home once again were we
to ask her for a change. We remembered that the title he chose fit
another piece and caused her to tighten her reins on originality:
she organized his dreams and the reality on the bookshelf where
she organized his dreams. She was always there, writing over ev-
erything which she would rein in when tapped for idylls out be-
yond the blind pasteurization where genres confuse pronouns and
violence.

He theorized that they refused the offer so that they might retain
tenure; I, on the other hand, would never have apologized for such
desires as asking others to give words as gifts to me and the little
time I had to return to them. This was the very consequence of
such a silence – it was the sort of gain only noticeable by what it
lost because it did not translate the world, which was nevertheless
not held, like a hostage, at a distance, but so close that its voice
became indistinguishable from the fact that I was winded, and I
listened for the things that preceded his presentation with my pres-
ence. Time does not follow up his sentiment with a sentence be-
cause his offer still lacks reciprocity.

Although the vow to end continuance was literal, a literary ex-
ample thus proclaimed frequent lapses in freedom; I found my-
self being hunted in my dreams with uncomfortable associations
whose intimacy is forced as it is in rape. Then the roads expanded
to give me an example of how to expend energy in the like manner
of the wind which does not end and so must save itself from rep-
etition. I'd seen her speaking with the woman I hoped would have
a better chance of escaping this education; I had always thought
betting on the wages brought in by being wedded to the world
would neither wield vertical promises nor yield them to proper
trials.

Certainly, the areas where he hung his thumbs had been reinforced for a raw attitude. He lay his questions out across tables and chairs. Odd numbers faced down in maddening fashion, soon beckoning the sun with writing to call upon them for an increase in sustain, much like the time a guitarist twirled the knobs and waved. It was the decade of great guitar solos shooting out of the speakers, following the middle eights of mediocre singles.

Only when the computer was turned on and the finely meshed file mended would I be able to count again on the coin. My turns come too quickly for writing to accept me unchanged.

I didn't know who assisted Olga. The boy had returned to the scenery of his father's lengthy ascent into the accidental world of coincidence. So tired so as to let this day evaporate through escape, I retracted my earlier statement through a contradiction I was preparing myself to explain should the need to do so so arise before me in the coming week. Going around again becomes all the merrier when waiting is the precious subject indicating the direction to which words solemnly fly, en route to warmth like migratory mammals in search of a land where climaxes are easily exhausted.

She may very well have learned through her encounters with heroism that he was smaller than his image. His eyes steadied themselves. He fixed them precisely on the speaker and/or object at hand for the purpose of understanding himself all the more.

Redoubled for an effect, I stood against the doorway and pressed my hands into the frame's corners. His concerns for the past held sway over the entire present. This alarm holds my fear more tightly in its fist than the events which continue daily, where overturned dressers mark what ended the evenings, when I was allowed no rest; I was listening to screams and threats. The window held my emotional futility within its microcosmic frame.

Less music meant there was more time in which to think and construct jokes against the backdrop of the now less distant day. And this pointed towards the type of fatigue she means when she says the light backs away from us and is pink falling among grey confines. A broken machine occupies the cornfield; we near its operator and run our index fingers over the teeth used for delicate, deliberate extraction, a process much like the change that happens when I am finished writing. I look again for proof of positivity and find the narrator needs less emphasis. I learned from him that one could not avoid choices.

I was told by a smaller part of me that I wanted to feel. This meant I would battle once again for the past but not belittle it for progress or the kind of immunity I had been bludgeoned into buying with air. She lay on top of me and I disappeared. There the air is crystallized in an historical attitude towards inevitability and fully denies the very abilities which helped me to survive by letting my fear flutter far off and away. The more quickly the door closes, the less of a glimpse I have of what happens behind it even as I become aware that, as I write, I stood before its opening for many interminable minutes I am not yet reporting.

He was exercised by so many questions that he had time for few remarks as long as paragraphs. Writing is simple if it is only psychologically sound for the writer and dismisses the same possibilities of like neuroses in the reader, so he confined himself to sentences as if to say that he had arrived before me, earlier than the urgent morning.

Theory was a similar exercise minus the simplicity of daily situations. For this reason, more readers find the slogans appealing, and they visualize their many enemies as part of the self they never fully integrate at the workplace. I coupled this with the fixed structure of the world and found my translations to be approved when

the interstice showed me just how long I'd been attracted to dis-
tance. Now I sniff the rain while my fingers keep determining the
impartiality of time, all of which I equate with the space between
the personal paragraphs and sentimental technique. I suddenly
recalled that his philosophy hearkened back to the days when the
crisis of death set in, formed by smallish bombs floating heavily
above him until their weight broke him open with their rapid fire.

Vague scenes arose in sentences that writing permitted but didn't
simply present. This all points out my forum's extremities. I
wanted what I saw to come sharply into view for me, but the re-
quirements of memory needed to be fulfilled emotionally as well,
meaning that feeding the distinct operations of my scattered agen-
das caused me to write in a labor intensive manner and precluded
the playfulness of the non-figurative and water-based. I received
my pain in the space taken up by the daily diaristic jottings and
jolts.

She sighed at each sentence that illustrated the truth of lived theory.
Was this the kind of speechlessness where the ones who would
never read opened it to any given page and complained of how
hard it was to follow the narrator? Could these objections be eas-
ily refuted by the author's argument that the narrator was no more
present than the spaces between the distribution of its sentences?

I want to complete the page beside me. The sounds spin my way
inside the complex circle of psychological pleasure that analysis
puts forth.

I looked across the sky through the window towards the words in the evening, where I would, in time, climb the mercantile hills and face my own emotional crises with subtlety. This was the conservation, by which I maintained an equal balance between word and deed, that sustained me. I had played her a snippet of the noun which soon became subordinate to an abandoned name; the light traced this name down through the ages I am in the process of resurrecting. And as she can see, I still milk things infinitely. She said my movements looked lifeless because of the fact that writing does not have an easily recognizable face. The two of us left to debate my absence, we devoured the residual inflictions.

He slammed down the cover to cover up the fact that he was too late to meet me. I mistook his anger for a psychological condition wherein the ID substituted itself for the subject by becoming an ID card left for the ego at the door. Now the bouncer appeared; an investigator matched the blood to the unused tread. Treading water by way of words, it seems that writing is my memorial methodology, but it does not mimeograph the days as they pass for the ones who do not now know me. It sounds slow, is anxious in its slowness.

Her accent increased all aural imprints. She had white skin and seemed unholy somehow – all because of the way her demonic husband spoke to her. We identified him as the hero. We followed the paths his protagonist's traps set for us. Later, as he chased his young son through a labyrinth, he froze to death because his son tricked him into the same wrong footsteps. As a result of my own brush with death, I shuddered when the axe struck through the door, since I had closed that very same door on them and did not wish to see this returning to the external world.

This was also aloof. Here I mean the way the building acquired a kind of ahistorical meaning framed in the narrative as a perfect example of unconscious repetition. But the man didn't see this game and, because of this blindness (which was imposed upon him), he became its most moveable pawn. He had always been there, and the servant, as well.

She stood on the stoop to stop me from advancing into the dark air, the force being so majestic we found ourselves crouching, for we needed to catch it without the possibility of falling back once again. But it was not magic. I was hiding my descriptions behind the way I held my body. I was always thinking more about how I spoke with hostility because I had only heard ideas presented as arguments at the table, vehemence dribbling on the stacked plates. So I let this experience affix me to mystery. And yet I felt a sort of wordless hysteria one normally associates with mimes – how their bodies are trapped both in the boxes their movements utilize for effect and the clothing outlasting muscular edges. These edges are also part of the artistic effect normally fulfilled by athletics, here reconfigured to disorder our competitiveness. I recounted the beginner's book I'd been reading to her. In this book miming and writing are as closely linked as creation and mimicry, for where does one begin while the other fades away against the background rearing out from the moment in which ashes and tears tear holes in the blank canvas from an immeasurable distance?

She found my remarks too impossible to comment upon and so speak to. But my time was commensurate with experience, as many days had passed over me while my idle pen died hard in the process of whittling sticks of words.

When I entered the room, she was quietly rejecting patterns of behaviour. I slowly stepped across the rug like I had when afraid of the violence in the next room, and I had projected this fear into water that still imagistically exists.

I extended myself while making myself seem less available. This was a further exemplification of how living alone reverberated throughout the papers they were to turn over to me when they finished learning the ferocity of language games. All this was to pierce the walls. Later, I lined them with questions and polls over an impromptu engagement. Out of everything I had yet to say, the issues ranging across the intimate and uncharted land between us were certainly the most urgently unformed paragraphs.

Someone unknowingly knocked. And then I learned that cars do not "hiss" when they pass – a sound only describable when images of animals are left alone and the night immediately employs the view. This is now silence as I am trying to negotiate it in a language stripped of images, a language settled in the dust the vacuum disposes of for company. But I won't bring this with me as we prepare to join more company. The invitation was indecisive and divisible by the number of people welcomed minus the number who could actually fit around the table. We knocked knees nervously together under the table.

The crowd spilled into the courtyard, being too large to fit on the roof and eat in comfort. I was asked if I, too, would participate in the cannibalistic activity. But I was much too young to decide how I felt about entering the bodies of others, even though my own body responded with affirmations I still encounter as an insomniac filled with fear when the light is lowered. Writing does not dumb experience down because language is too intelligent to make a pen ignorant of events. Is this an applicable theory of the novel, or is it a more suitable fit for a poetic moment that puts grace in process?

We had to wash our hands to attain distance from the grease and the time around it. And yet we were working in such a way that our hands did not need to be clean, for the materials nearly choked us with the dust we brought with us up into the light. I remember that she had turned the light off when she came close to me. It was too dark for me to see her face; I may have also cast the image in black to forget it until I turned old enough to flesh it out as writing and to feel it inside who I was as an adult.

Entrancing us with a kind of immanent wisdom we were able to notice only now, stepping out the door and into the nearly blank day, the past flashed before the two of us in the service of narrative fiction, so writing a novel became the strictest form of autobiography because it wrote itself presently.

She is wasting the destructive parts of herself on the pillow. This object has the convenience she was hoping for, waiting as she was for the days to move around the object. This is also to tell you that memory, while subjective, is not the thing that determines the body for me; it is the body that instructs me to look towards the past. But here I no longer mean the past as it is what we no longer are.

We were learning that one could enter the day through diurnal events blocking us from seeing more of each other. We saw the traumas before us, and writing helped us to enforce their impact at each moment while debunking the minutiae of each minute, the essence of meaning made mobile by writing, pushing the combined sections of the mobile in a slow cycle. Would a thinker accept our rotating ideas as part of the poem, the parcel as yet unopened by or penned upon this page?

We wanted to spend the day in the service of art, surrounded by silence. We found the sounds of breathing scattered across the surface. This was a way of joining in the activity without pretending we knew anything about it, as I, myself, do not speak of aesthetics like that. And yet my comments did not buttonhole the meaning of art – each of us used color in radically different ways, none of which expressed what I might call my physical space.

Writing (I am now thinking of this) seemed more physical than painting because the voice it hinted at, even if independent of a body, was itself bodily by definition, for sound is always symptomatic of the world where we lay down our fingers and sympathetic to the energy I use for pointing out objects. He seemed to understand the motive of my writing, a reasoning based on the clarity of parataxis. I jumped ahead among fictive events.

And yet I was behind in everything because I overidentified with the feminine, leaving the self outside the subjectivity I knew I was here to love. Was my hunger a metaphor for writing, a mode of operation that shut down my unyielding devices?

She is behind the locked door, and so I am safe. The corroboration I seek is not left to the man who can only devastate through deviation; this is a form of forensic activity.

The second man put his hand into the fragments to feel the flames and incurred an injury at the level of defining his circuitous self in circular terms. The language I wanted him to use seemed far away, as if the night held us at a great distance while I watched something try to rise, then going awry and falling in esteemed failure. I did not pay attention. I then realized that writing was negligible when it came to the others I'd observed as being in agreement – agreement meant the novel was a promise towards the world made in concord with narrative, a link too broadly associated with assumed noise. I wished for no such affiliations with him, association being little more than a dull ringing in the ears of the other. The screen shut itself up far away from me when I said I knew the ending. I did not speak so loudly. I spoke in the voice of the novel for the purpose of tuning autobiography to an essentially poetic pitch.

And it would be so much easier in minutes: I had decided to let the opening slide me back into the outside world. And I wanted the darkness I would encounter there. Yet this is not to say that I would then find complete satisfaction, since the leather collar eventually focused us away from intimacy – in fact, choking it off entirely. Would I report my findings in a pose, or would it be better for me to prepare myself for the possession positioned on the next page?

These returns retire the illusion of writing as a negligible practice, and yet it is easy to see, plodding ahead into the prescribed emptiness, that it is words, and not the characteristic deeds acted out by plotlines, which grant my illicit permission. This is to say that existence allows me to alter the pronouns because I am demanded to do so in the service of sentences, all of which the pen sends into a cleanliness sparkling with grit.

The book was authored by the same man who divulged the crime of literature to me, the indulgence of a kind of simplistic vulgarity. Hanging over the washer was an immense web; the same puzzlement caused the hero to tremble and shout.

The eyes serve the fatigued signal. And so these signs suggest other subliminalities. She was pulling away from me to publish her dislike of the subject; she looked more philosophical than ever. Her message was such that when I moved my mouth, my motives were no longer questionable, as truth seemed to dazzle us at the very center of our elephantine wisdom. We stood and huddled against the source. But we didn't stand up.

To tremble was like asking opposition to sit down across from me and grimace. I thought of my father very quickly, but not quite immediately.

The cold air beckoned. But for whom was this call intended when it was difficult to see who else was also in the room? Is it also likely that the screen was there only for her to place herself in the ghastly glow of the beckoning meadow, as it was there that her dreams met explanations more solidly than in the lobby?

Her sicknesses were not feigned, she assured me, just mistaken for my sake. I turned away as the focus surged towards her seeming cause; I had declared delays inherent in placing propositions so squarely before me. She, too, disengaged herself from the demeanor of overwork, the demarcation being drawn out along the vocation she had set out for herself, for here she could put tables and chairs where they hadn't been laid out in childhood. I was holding myself aloof from her revelations for this very purpose.

It now seems I supplant these images with everything coming in from the North, traversing a giant distance – one large enough to force me to say "speech", as this is the meridian I seize.

When does writing return my face?